HOW T

BEAT

MINECRAFT

MORTIMER

Published in 2023 by Mortimer Children's
An Imprint of Welbeck Children's Limited,
part of the Welbeck Publishing Group
Offices in: London - 20 Mortimer Street, London W1T 3JW
& Sydney - 205 Commonwealth Street, Surry Hills 2010
www.welbeckpublishing.com

All information correct as of January 2023.

ISBN: 978 1 83935 235 5

Printed in Heshan, China

3 5 7 9 10 8 6 4 2

Designed, written, and packaged by: Dynamo Limited
Designer: Sam James
Editorial Manager: Joff Brown
Production: Melanie Robertson

FSC
www.fsc.org
MIX
Paper | Supporting
responsible forestry
FSC® C020056

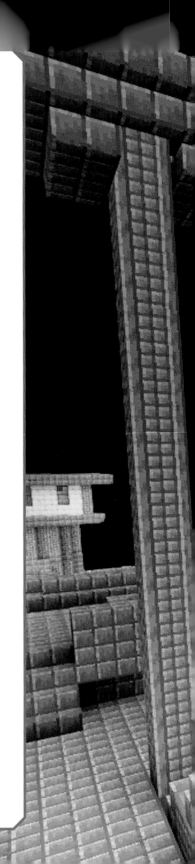

HOW TO BEAT MINECRAFT

CONTENTS

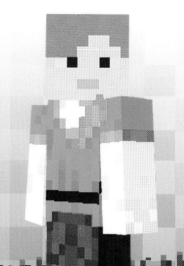

WELCOME TO THE
MINECRAFT WORLD!

Blocks, mobs, biomes, crafting, farming, creepers, enchantments . . . these epic things are all part of the awesome world of Minecraft!

It's one of the biggest games ever, and if these words already mean something to you, then you know a little about it. But don't worry if it's all completely new because this awesome book will reveal everything you need to become a Minecraft master!

Amazing Adventures

Minecraft lets you have amazing adventures in incredible landscapes. You will play in different locations, from forests and mountains to deserts and oceans. You will need to mine blocks, craft items, explore locations, stay healthy, defeat enemies, and much more in order to survive and progress. Each time you play, you learn something new and gain experience. Minecraft is fun and totally unique!

Minecraft Modes

Minecraft has different modes of play. In Creative mode, you have all the blocks and items that you want, monsters won't attack, and there's no need to eat. In Survival mode, you must mine, collect, and craft to stay alive. Plus, you'll need to explore, battle enemies, and look after your health and hunger bar. **This book is all about how to beat Minecraft in single-player Survival mode**. It's packed full of tips, guides, hints, and secrets that will turn you from a noob into a pro player!

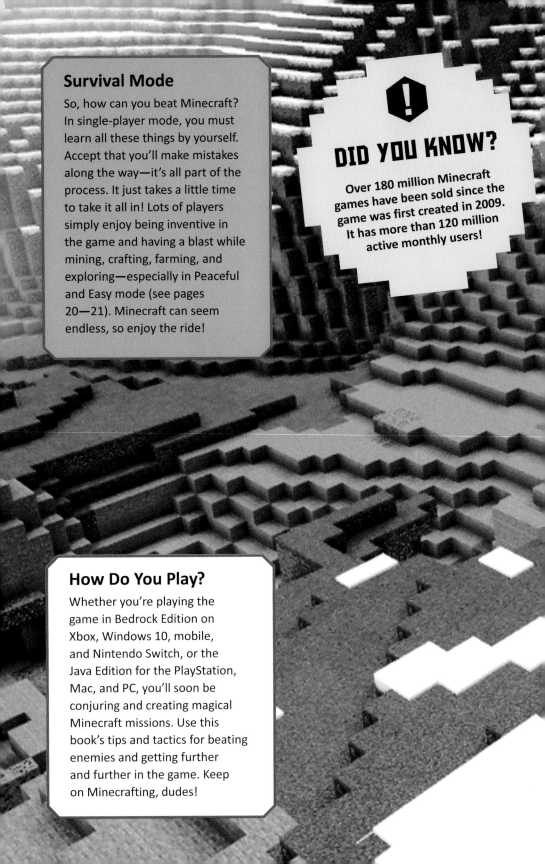

Survival Mode

So, how can you beat Minecraft?
In single-player mode, you must
learn all these things by yourself.
Accept that you'll make mistakes
along the way—it's all part of the
process. It just takes a little time
to take it all in! Lots of players
simply enjoy being inventive in
the game and having a blast while
mining, crafting, farming, and
exploring—especially in Peaceful
and Easy mode (see pages
20—21). Minecraft can seem
endless, so enjoy the ride!

DID YOU KNOW?

Over 180 million Minecraft
games have been sold since the
game was first created in 2009.
It has more than 120 million
active monthly users!

How Do You Play?

Whether you're playing the
game in Bedrock Edition on
Xbox, Windows 10, mobile,
and Nintendo Switch, or the
Java Edition for the PlayStation,
Mac, and PC, you'll soon be
conjuring and creating magical
Minecraft missions. Use this
book's tips and tactics for beating
enemies and getting further
and further in the game. Keep
on Minecrafting, dudes!

Survival Champion

As you play more and your confidence rises, the thought of venturing from the Overworld (the place where all your adventures begin) to the dangerous dimension of the Nether will become more appealing. Venture into the deep dark and encounter deadlier enemies such as the warden. Finally, you'll be brave enough to visit the End and come face to face with the ender dragon! Defeating her is the ultimate achievement in becoming a Minecraft Survival champion.

MYSTERIOUS MINECRAFT?

Minecraft might seem confusing at first, but is it too brain-busting to understand? Of course not!

Developers Mojang have made it very easy to get started when you follow a few basics, with updates keeping the game fresh. There are more taxing tasks once you know the ins and outs, too. As long as you survive and stay alive, there's no right or wrong way to play.

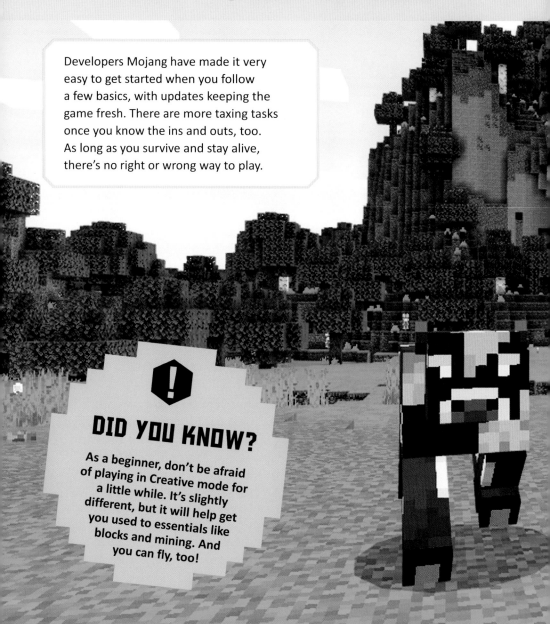

! DID YOU KNOW?

As a beginner, don't be afraid of playing in Creative mode for a little while. It's slightly different, but it will help get you used to essentials like blocks and mining. And you can fly, too!

Blocks and Tools

You'll soon learn how to break and mine blocks with certain tools, and you'll figure out that items like food and armor can be collected from drops or crafted yourself. Your experience points are earned when you mine, defeat mobs (short for "mobiles" and meaning any moving thing, whether friendly or evil), breed animals, and use furnaces. These "XP" will boost your levels and be used to craft enchanted tools, armor and weapons.

You'll use things such as ores, pickaxes, torches, villages, smelting, shelters, and potions as you build up your Minecraft expertise and intelligence. Exciting new developments added way after the game's first release (pillagers, bamboo, crossbows, pandas, and shipwrecks) make the gameplay even more interesting.

STEP 1— GET STARTED

From getting started in a Minecraft Survival world
to basic controls, settings, blocks, items and exploration,
this section reveals all the simple stuff you need to know.
You'll catch a glimpse of the Nether and the End, and even
some helpful naturally generated structures. It's time to learn
a lot of essential info!

SAY HELLO TO . . . YOU!

When you start a game, you can take control of Steve or Alex, the legendary characters that represent you in the Minecraft world!

Skins

Players choose to play as either of these cool characters, also known as skins. Steve is probably more famous, having been in the game right from the start, with Alex having arrived as an option in 2014. She's a bit slimmer in the arms than Steve and quickly became an icon for gamers!

Steve and Alex

Steve and Alex are 1.8 blocks tall and 0.6 blocks wide. They walk at around 4.3 blocks per second, with the ability to walk just over 5,000 blocks in a single day in Minecraft. The characters can also sprint, boosting their speed to 5.6 blocks, but this can't be done if your hunger bar is at three or lower. Sprinting zaps your hunger quicker than walking does.

DID YOU KNOW?

Character Creator, an option in the Bedrock Edition, lets players customize their skin's size and shape, eyes, mouth, skin tone, hairstyle, and more!

Time

Time passes much faster in Minecraft. A day is 20 minutes long, with 10 minutes for daytime and seven minutes for nighttime. There are 1.5 minutes each for sunset and sunrise.

DID YOU KNOW?

There's no on-screen clock to tell you the time. A clock can be crafted to show the sun and moon's positions, which is very helpful if you're underground.

TAKE CONTROL

Understanding which buttons control your character and all the options at your fingertips is not as tricky as you may think. Discover what you need to know right here!

Control Settings

All control settings are displayed on the Minecraft home screen. Here, console, desktop, and handheld players will discover important moves, such as how to place and use an item, mine, access the inventory and crafting menus, dropping, jumping, throwing, and more.

PLAY

SETTINGS

MARKETPLACE

NEW

PROFILE

Settings
Click here to get to your control settings.

HUD

Get familiar with your heads-up display (the HUD), and its function on your screen.

Health

These 10 hearts form the health bar, with a red heart representing two health points (20 in total). Health takes a hit when you don't eat, or if you suffer damage such as falling or enemy attacks.

Crosshairs

The cross, or plus sign, is your crosshairs. It shows exactly where you'll make contact with a block using the item or tool in your hand. It's also handy for being accurate when aiming at enemies!

XP

This shows your experience (see page 10).

Hotbar

These nine boxes make up your hotbar. Keep important things here, such as food and torches, so you can access them quickly. The hotbar is always on display.

Hunger Bar

The 10 tasty drumsticks show your hunger bar, with a maximum of 20 hunger rating (two per drumstick). Activities such as sprinting and combat will drain hunger, which then loses health points. When the hunger bar is 18 or higher, health can regenerate.

INSIDE YOUR
INVENTORY

You'll need a good understanding of how your inventory works and what it does. Luckily, it's all explained here for you!

Open Your inventory

To open your inventory, just tap the Y button on Xbox and Switch, the triangle on PlayStation, the E key on keyboard, and the triple-dot button on mobile devices. The inventory is vital to your survival and progression. It allows you to craft, select armor, equip tools, and store the cool stuff that you discover.

Storage Slots

There are 27 **storage slots** (also known as **item slots**). Here, you can keep food, weapons, blocks, tools, and everything else for your adventures. Many things can be "stacked" in each slot, to a maximum value of 64.

Hotbar Slot

In the **hotbar** slots, whatever is selected will be used in your main hand.

Character Skin

This is an image of your character skin (just in case you ever forget what you look like!).

Crafting Grid

This is your **crafting grid**. You'll learn more about this from page 38 onward, but this is the place to start simple crafting.

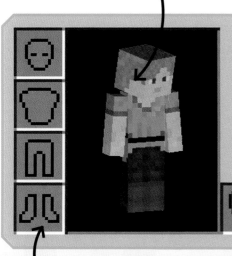

Armor Slots

The four **armor slots** are great for when you need protection from hostile mobs. Armor consists of a helmet, chestplate, leggings, and boots.

Off-Hand Slot

If there's nothing in your selected hotbar slot, the off-hand slot will automatically be used.

DID YOU KNOW?

Select the "?" symbol at the top of the inventory for a very detailed guide to loads of information, including crafting and farming.

DIFFICULT DECISIONS!

When you begin a Minecraft Survival game, you have the choice of picking a difficulty level for your world in the settings option.

Easy

Go for an "easy" life, and you are at risk of mobs attacking, but the level of damage dealt is much less than in Normal setting. Unlike in Peaceful, hunger can be depleted. Spending your early Minecraft days in this option is very wise, since you'll still come face to face with zombies and skeletons, for example, but suffer less harm.

Peaceful

Want a quiet and totally stress-free adventure? Choose Peaceful and you'll be in total heaven! In this difficulty, there are no hostile mobs to attack you, and your health bar regenerates very quickly. There's no need to eat because the hunger bar will remain at max. Beginners can get a lot from this mode, and it's nice to know that a scary creature won't come after you!

Normal

Here's where the playing field is leveled! Usual Minecraft rules now apply, meaning damage levels from mobs are at the Regular setting, and hunger and health operate just as you would expect. This is the most popular world option for everyday players who are anxious to see how they cope in the 'real' world, with real problems and enemies.

Hard

Let's turn up the jeopardy, yeah? Switch to Hard and keep scanning for danger, since mob attacks have greater damage. You'll also find irritating details, such as zombies being able to break wooden doors, and you can die from hunger. It's a tough existence in Hard mode, but take it on, and you'll prove your Survival skills!

STEP 2—OVERWORLD OVERLOAD

Your Minecraft adventure will kick off in the Overworld—a vast and exciting place containing many different types of environment. This section explains how it's generated, what it's made of, and what you can expect to find there. From basic blocks to surprising structures, here's the ultimate whistle-stop tour!

GENERATION GAME

And in the beginning, there were blocks.

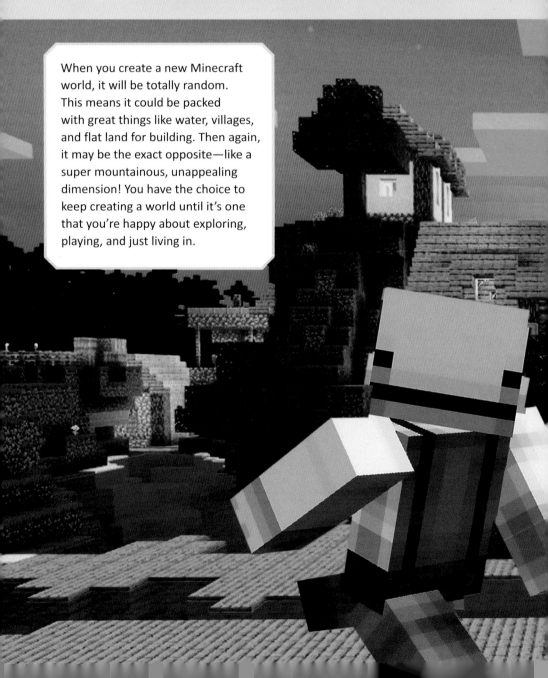

When you create a new Minecraft world, it will be totally random. This means it could be packed with great things like water, villages, and flat land for building. Then again, it may be the exact opposite—like a super mountainous, unappealing dimension! You have the choice to keep creating a world until it's one that you're happy about exploring, playing, and just living in.

Seeds

Each world has something called a **seed**. They're random identification numbers assigned to every individual world. If you know of a seed that you'd like to visit, you can enter it into the settings section.

Chunks

As you explore, **chunks** of the Overworld generate around you. Chunks are 16 blocks wide, 16 long, and 256 high. The more you wander, the more chunks will appear around you.

Coordinates

Your exact location in the Overworld can be determined by your **coordinates**. Measured from your spawn point (the spot at which you reappear after dying), there's an x axis (east to west location), z axis (your north to south location) and y axis (how low or high you are). In Minecraft we measure space in blocks, so if we talk about something being 64 on the y axis, we mean it's 64 blocks above that spawn point. In Bedrock, coordinates can be switched on through the settings section.

TYPES OF BIOME

In the Overworld, there are lots of different landscapes and places you can spawn in and venture to. These are distinct regions called biomes. It's time for a tour of the pluses and minuses of each!

Plains

GOOD FOR . . . beginners, because plains are flat (good for building) and frequently have villages. Sunflower plains look super-pretty!

BAD FOR . . . wood fans, since trees are a real rarity.

Forest

GOOD FOR . . . getting wood for crafting! There are different forest types, including birch, dark, and flower.

BAD FOR . . . letting in light. Dark and dense forests are a great place for hostile mobs to spawn and lurk.

Jungle

GOOD FOR . . . finding exclusive items and mobs like ocelots, parrots, melons, bamboo, pandas, and cocoa.

BAD FOR . . . new players. Jungles are thick and well-covered, with danger potentially hiding in the shade!

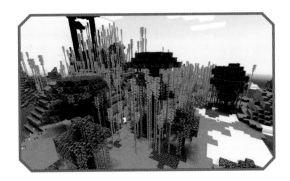

Savanna

GOOD FOR . . . dry weather, tall grass, and flat land for a beginner to build on.

BAD FOR . . . farming, because the land and weather is just not cut out for it.

Mountains

GOOD FOR . . . mining rare emerald ore! Mountains can be wooded, gravelly, or stony with lots of features.

BAD FOR . . . fall damage. There's always a risk of tumbling dowm the steep sides and uneven surfaces.

Caves

GOOD FOR . . . finding rare plants and animals in lush caves, and Ancient Cities in the deep dark.

BAD FOR . . . hostile mobs. They spawn everywhere in the darkness, and the warden is the toughest of them all!

See "STEP 14—NEW HEIGHTS AND DEPTHS" for more on cave and mountain sub-biomes!

Swamp

GOOD FOR . . . fishing, trees, mushrooms, sugar cane, clay, and sand.

BAD FOR . . . drowned mobs, causing not-so-pleasant nights around this dark-green biome!

Badlands

GOOD FOR . . . abandoned mineshafts— they generate much closer to the surface, and you can sometimes find them in the open air.

BAD FOR . . . growing food—besides uneven surfaces, you won't find much in the way of trees, grass, or water here.

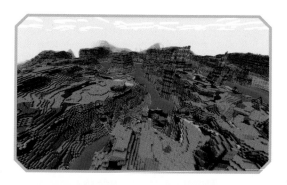

Desert

GOOD FOR . . . a challenge, because deserts are difficult to establish in! It's easy to spot hostile mobs since it's so open, with little cover.

BAD FOR . . . farming and mining.

Windswept Hills

GOOD FOR . . . spectacular views— floating islands and high waterfalls often generate in this biome.

BAD FOR . . . silverfish. When mining here, there's a higher chance of striking infested stone.

Beach

GOOD FOR . . . buried treasure. This is the most likely place to find it, more likely than on the ocean floor.

BAD FOR . . . resources. There's not much of anything here!

Taiga

GOOD FOR . . . trees, since it's a forest-like biome. Includes snowy terrains and flat lands packed with spruce trees.

BAD FOR . . . building and climbing in the higher mountainous areas. Watch out for wolves, too!

Ocean

GOOD FOR . . . experienced players who like a quest, and perhaps a bit of squid! There's a big selection of ocean types, from warm and shallow to frozen and deep.

BAD FOR . . . building!

Mushroom Island

GOOD FOR . . . exploring! Only mooshrooms will spawn naturally on this landscape and no dangerous mobs.

BAD FOR . . . those who actually want to locate it because this biome is rare!

THE NETHER AND THE END

This is where your world gets super serious, because the Nether and the End are two terrifying dimensions! Here's a quick look at exactly why that is . . .

Nether Portal

With mobs like ghasts, wither skeletons, and blazes, the Nether's dark and lava-laced cliffs are a sight like nothing you'll have witnessed in the Overworld! To enter it, you'll need to build a Nether portal from obsidian, then be prepared for the dangers on the other side of it.

The Nether

The Nether is a crucial part of Minecraft. Here, you can craft potions and collect essential blaze rods, which are key to locating a stronghold and then accessing the End! Nether fortresses are natural structures discovered in the Nether. They're stuffed with loot chests and vital blaze spawners.

The End

The End may not appear as terrifying as the Nether, but these barren, near resourceless islands are suitable only for the most expert players. Your task—the ultimate Minecraft mission—is to take on the ender dragon and then escape to the outer islands.

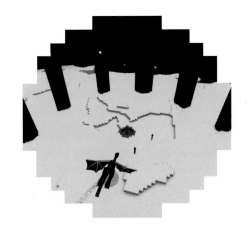

The void, end stone, shulkers, endermen, and (hopefully!) the dragon egg await you in this legendary dimension. You'll need good guidance, tactics, and a little bit of luck as you take on the End and everything it throws at you. There's more about these two mysterious environments later on!

BRILLIANT BLOCKS

Blocks are all around you in Minecraft. They make up the landscape, they allow you to build, and you can collect them and craft your own.

Grass, dirt, stone, lava, and water are all blocks. Different blocks will have different appearances, and they can be a solid or a liquid. Some blocks will do a specific job—for example, a chest block stores items. Some blocks drop an item when broken, such as a bookshelf dropping books and coal ore dropping coal. Clearly, blocks are totally awesome!

DID YOU KNOW?

Blocks such as iron ore and copper ore drop raw metal when mined—unless you use the Silk Touch enchantment!

Breaking Blocks

Breaking blocks with your hand or a specific tool causes them to break into smaller pieces, which you can then pick up. Tools are quicker at breaking blocks. An axe collects wood, and the pickaxe will mine ores, rock, and metal blocks. Did you know that there's even a note block? It plays a musical sound when it's hit!

A few block types you should know:

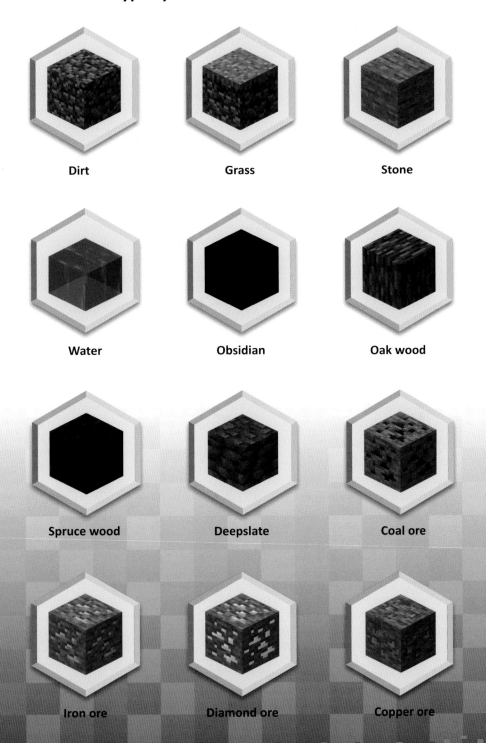

Dirt

Grass

Stone

Water

Obsidian

Oak wood

Spruce wood

Deepslate

Coal ore

Iron ore

Diamond ore

Copper ore

EPIC ITEMS

Items are similar to blocks, and are a core gameplay function. You'll soon need to craft some items, so check out this mini guide.

Tools, weapons, food, armor . . . these are all types of items. There are hundreds in Minecraft Survival. Ways to collect items include picking them up after they're dropped by mobs, finding a loot chest, or crafting them yourself. Items can be stored in your inventory for use in your world when needed.

Starter Items

A pickaxe, axe, sword, and shovel are useful items to have in your inventory early in a game. Later on, items such as a bucket, bowl, ladder, bow, and even gunpowder will help you get further and survive after regular contact with hostile attacking mobs.

Mobs

Mobs are a great source of items, which they can drop when defeated and even when they're alive. Passive (friendly), neutral (either friendly or nasty), and hostile (nasty) mobs will all do this. Sheep, for example, will drop wool when they're alive, then drop meat after being killed. Horses will drop all of their equipment when they die, which could include a chest and saddle.

Some useful items:

Axe	Stick	Apple
Sword	Bucket	Wheat
Map	Bowl	Compass
Flint and steel	Wooden hoe	Shovel

QUICK GUIDE

Here's a handy list to show you some of the popular and most useful items and blocks around.

 Anvil

 Bamboo

 Baked potato

 Banner

 Barrel

 Bed

 Blast furnace

 Blaze rod

 Boat

 Bone

 Boots

 Bow

 Bread

 Brewing stand

 Cake

 Carpet

 Carrot

 Charcoal

 Chest

 Chestplate

 Clock

 Cobblestone

 Composter

 Concrete

 Concrete powder

 Cooked chicken

 Crafting table

 Crossbow

 Diamond axe

 Dye

 Egg

 Enchanted book

 Enchantment table

 Ender chest

 Ender pearl

 Feather

 Fence

 Fence gate

 Fishing rod

 Furnace

 Glass

 Glass bottle

Gravel

 Grindstone

 Gunpowder

 Helmet

 Hopper

 Iron ingot

 Kelp

 Ladder

 Leggings

 Lilac

 Lily pad

 Loom

 Magma

 Minecart

 Mushroom

 Mycelium

 Oak door

 Oak fence

 Paper

 Peony

 Pickaxe

 Podzol

 Pumpkin pie

 Red sandstone

 Redstone

 Rose bush

 Saddle

 Sapling

 Seagrass

 Sea lantern

 Shears

 Shield

 Shulker box

 Sign

 Smoker

 Snow

 Stonecutter

 Steak

 String

 Sunflower

 Sugar

 Sugar cane

 TNT

 Torch

 Totem of Undying

 Trapdoor

 Wall

 Wool

GETTING AROUND

The openness of a Minecraft world makes it easy to get lost—but there are tools to help . . .

A Helpful Pointer

The most basic item to help you get around is a compass. You can craft one using four iron ingots and some redstone dust. There's also a pretty good chance of finding one in a village, inside a cartographer's chest.

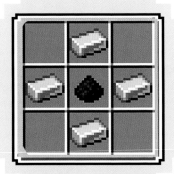

Clever Cartography

Cartographers' chests also often contain maps. Alternatively, with eight pieces of paper and a compass, you can craft a map. As you travel around, the map will fill with information about the area— but you have to be holding the map for this to work.

See "STEP 3—SURVIVE 24 HOURS" for more on crafting.

Note that the center of a map is not the place where it was created, as you might expect. Your Minecraft world is divided into a large invisible grid, and the map will detail whichever square it was created in.

New Directions

If a compass is used on a lodestone, then it becomes a lodestone compass and will always point to that lodestone. So if you build a lodestone into your house, for example, you can always find your way back there. A lodestone can be crafted from eight chiseled stone bricks and a netherite ingot. A recovery compass is another useful tool that can be crafted from a compass and eight echo shards. It points toward the spot where the player last died—utterly invaluable when you die in some obscure valley miles from home and want to get your loot back.

NATURALLY GENERATING STRUCTURES

The structures in the following pages can appear around your world and have lots of useful resources to explore and benefits to reap!

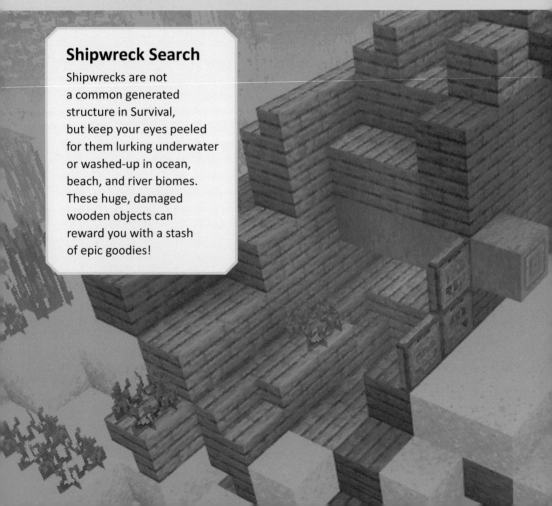

Shipwreck Search

Shipwrecks are not a common generated structure in Survival, but keep your eyes peeled for them lurking underwater or washed-up in ocean, beach, and river biomes. These huge, damaged wooden objects can reward you with a stash of epic goodies!

Hidden Treasure

A shipwreck can contain one, two, or three chests depending on its size. They'll either be a map chest, treasure chest, or supply chest. Search the vessel's labyrinth of rooms to uncover these prized boxes.

Follow That Dolphin!

If you feed a dolphin raw cod or raw salmon, they will lead you to a secret shipwreck.

On the Map

A map chest is a great thing to find in a shipwreck because it has a 100% chance of containing a buried treasure map. They belong to a sub-category of maps called explorer maps, and the buried treasure map only generates underwater—they can also be found in underwater ruins. The map's white dot shows the direction you're facing and leads you to the magic red cross. When you're above the buried treasure, dig down and reveal the chest's haul of items, which should be gold, emeralds, swords, and food. You'll feel like a legit pirate now!

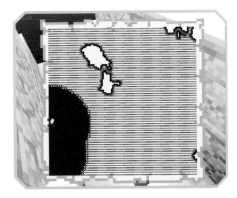

Welcome to Our Village

Villages generate pretty commonly, and if you've played any Survival Mode, you've probably encountered one already. They generate in several types of flat, open biome, such as plains, savanna, snowy plains, and desert. Villages are inhabited by villagers, but they have a 2% chance of generating as abandoned villages inhabited by zombie villagers.

Further Exploration

Besides the buried treasure map, two other types of explorer maps are available—woodland and ocean. The ocean explorer map is sold by apprentice cartographer villagers and costs one compass and 13 emeralds. You'll need one extra emerald to buy the woodland explorer map from journeyman cartographers. The map shows the outline of land and water, and indicates where a woodland mansion or an ocean monument is located. As you move around, it will fill in like a normal map.

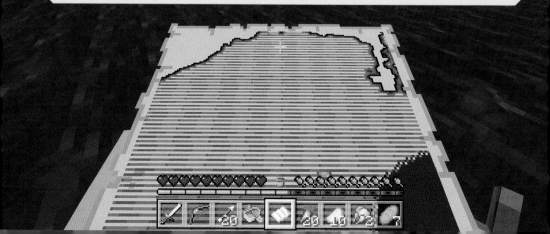

Country House

Woodland mansions are rare—they generate in dark forest biomes, usually a long way from the world's original spawn point. They always have three floors, but randomly generate with a variety of rooms, and will be inhabited by vindicators, evokers, and allays, as well as other hostile mobs that spawn in darkness. Killing an evoker will give you a totem of undying, and there's good loot to be found in woodland mansion chests.

Sunken Structures

Ocean monuments are large, ancient-looking buildings that spawn in deep ocean biomes. They don't contain loot chests, but they're the only source of sponges and one of only two sources of prismarine. Each monument contains three elder guardians and is also the only place where guardians spawn.

Ruin Reconnaissance

The other place to find prismarine is in ocean ruins. It can spawn in all types of ocean biome and may occasionally spawn on beaches. Cold ocean ruins are mostly made of stone bricks, while warmer biomes and beaches will have a mix of sandstone and stone ruins. Loot chests are commonly found here.

Hit the Hut

Swamp huts, as you might expect, will sometimes generate in swamps. They're made of spruce planks and are inhabited by witches. You'll find a cauldron and crafting table inside. If you're playing the Bedrock Edition, the cauldron will have a random potion inside.

Get to the Point

Pyramids—often called temples—generate in desert and jungle. The desert variant is made of sandstone and has the traditional pyramid shape: some of the structure may be buried in the sand. The jungle version is made of cobblestone, some of it mossy. Both contain loot, but the desert pyramid is equipped with a TNT trap, while the jungle one has a puzzle and tripwires.

That's Mine

Mineshafts—often referred to as abandoned mineshafts—can sometimes be found in caves, and consist of tunnels, wooden platforms and supports, and fragments of rail track. Loot chests can often be found in them. Mines also generate overground in badlands biomes, and they're a good source of gold.

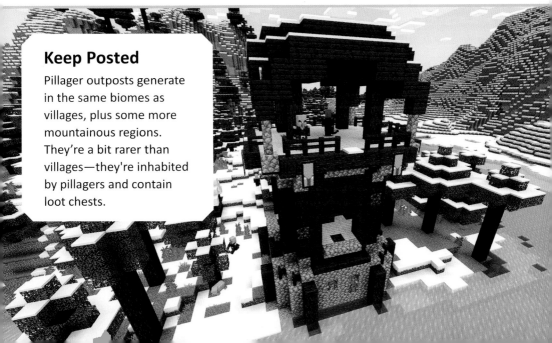

Keep Posted

Pillager outposts generate in the same biomes as villages, plus some more mountainous regions. They're a bit rarer than villages—they're inhabited by pillagers and contain loot chests.

STEP 3— SURVIVE 24 HOURS

So you can mine essential blocks, craft and use basic items, and recognize some helpful natural structures in your Survival world. Now it's important to check out this advanced advice on surviving your first day and preparing for more detailed exploring. Keep your eyes peeled for some epic extra instructions!

SURVIVING 24 HOURS:
24 TIPS

At the start of a new Minecraft adventure, it's important to act quickly to survive the first day. Follow these top tips . . .

1

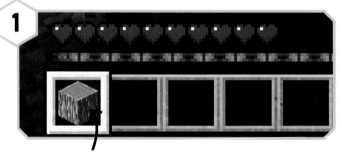

Start mining wood by using your hands to hit a tree. Try to collect at least 10 wood (logs).

The wood you mine will appear in your hotbar.

3

Use four wood planks in your grafting grid to make a crafting table. This is called a recipe. A recipe is anything you arrange in a crafting grid or table to create an output.

2

Then, drag wood from your inventory into your crafting grid. This will turn into wood planks.

Place the crafting table on the ground.

4 To mine blocks to make a shelter, you'll need tools. The first tool to make is a wooden pickaxe. A pickaxe needs sticks, which can be crafted by placing two planks in your crafting table, exactly like this.

5 A wooden pickaxe is crafted by arranging three planks and two sticks, exactly like this.

6 Before moving on to look for stone to mine, place your crafting table back in inventory. Otherwise, it will just stay on the ground where you left it!

DID YOU KNOW?

You will often have a stack of blocks with a small number in the corner showing how many you have. This can be split and dragged individually into your inventory boxes.

7 It's a good idea to look for a hill, so that you can mine stone and begin to make a shelter easily before darkness comes.

8 Using your pickaxe, begin to mine lots of cobblestone from the hill.

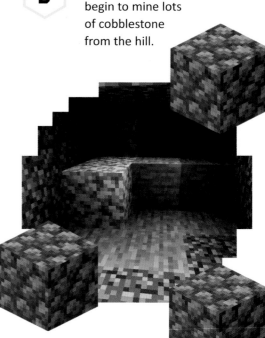

9 With stone blocks now in your inventory, you can craft a stone pickaxe by using this exact recipe. Remember that a stone pickaxe mines stone much more efficiently than a wooden pickaxe.

10

Planks and cobblestone can also be used in recipes to craft a stone sword, stone axe, and stone shovel.

11

If any animals are nearby, especially if you're near a village, you can kill some with a tool and collect the meat they drop for food (once cooked) later on.

12

This recipe using eight cobblestone allows you to craft a furnace, which cooks raw meat into cooked food for use when you're hungry.

13 A furnace also smelts things such as iron ore into iron ingot and logs into charcoal.

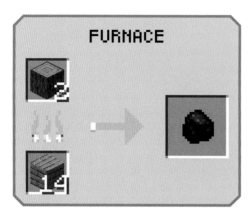

FURNACE

14 Coal ore blocks, which are gray with small black flecks, can be mined with a stone pickaxe. This will drop coal for use as a fuel in the furnace.

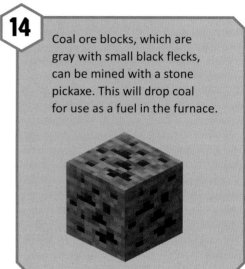

15 With your furnace on the ground, the fuel (coal) must go into the bottom slot, and then the meat goes in the top. Move cooked food to your inventory slots.

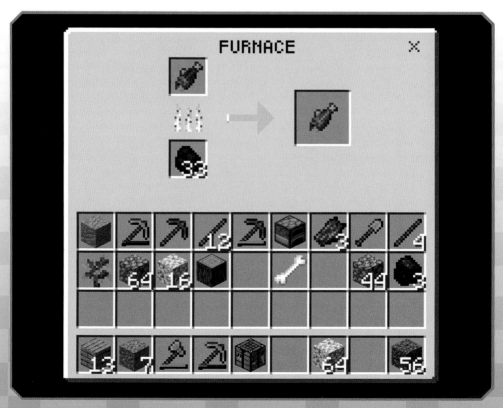

FURNACE

16 Your shelter, which you've mined into the side of the hill, will need lighting when it gets dark. Torches help you see in the dark and underground.

17 A torch is crafted by simply placing coal and a stick into a crafting recipe, exactly like this.

18 Harmful mobs will spawn when the light is reduced. Light levels range from 0 to 15, and creepers, zombies, and skeletons spawn at a level of seven or lower.

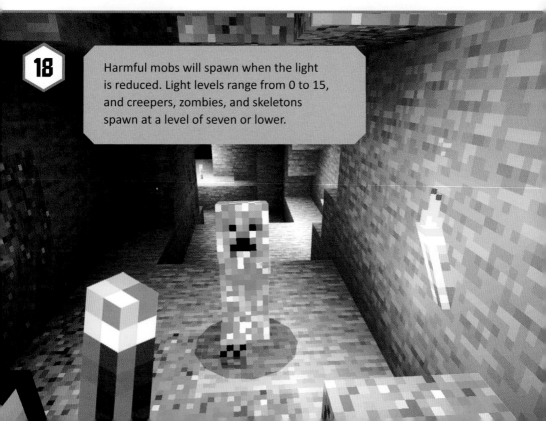

19 The hill mining you've done will create a small, quick shelter for you to hide in during the night.

20 Inside the shelter, you can even craft a wooden door to keep monsters out. Use this recipe in your crafting table.

21 The two extra doors that you have (six planks in a recipe like this always make three doors) could be used as fuel in the furnace.

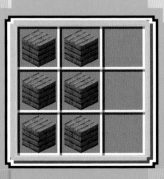

22 When a sheep is killed, it will drop wool. Three wool blocks and three planks are needed to craft a bed.

23 Sleeping in your shelter keeps you away from nasty mobs. After sleeping in a bed, it will be your spawn point if you're unlucky enough to die!

24

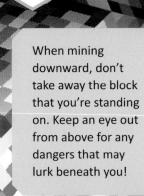

When mining downward, don't take away the block that you're standing on. Keep an eye out from above for any dangers that may lurk beneath you!

TAKE SHELTER

Check out these simple ways to enhance your shelter. It's time to get houseproud!

Building Materials

Cobblestone, wood, dirt, and stone bricks are all good blocks to use to build a safe structure on flat land for sheltering inside. It doesn't have to be complicated—something that's around 10 blocks by 10 blocks will be fine. Remember to put a roof across—the spider mob can climb walls and do you damage! Always add a door, because unless you're playing in Hard difficulty, zombie mobs can't break them down.

Fence Crafting

With your crafting table placed inside your shelter, you can begin crafting a fence using this recipe. Fence blocks can be placed around the front of your shelter to protect your door and entrance/exit area—most mobs won't be able to jump the fence! Preexisting fence blocks can also be mined from villages and are very useful in farming. Place a carpet tile (see pages 90—91) on the fence as a smart way to help you jump the fence!

Luxurious Shelter

If you're after a slightly more luxurious-looking shelter, try adding a sloped roof instead of a flat one. This will give you a little more room inside. Wood stairs can actually be used as a sneaky roof! They can be crafted by placing six planks in your crafting table, with one plank in the top left corner and two in the second row, leaving the third space free and three in the bottom row. You'll find more about shelters from page 88.

DID YOU KNOW?

You can make the most basic shelter simply by mining three blocks down . . . then jumping in and putting a block above you! To get out, you can repeat jumping and placing a block.

INSIDER INFO

You can sleep inside your shelter at night, but don't completely waste the time that you have while hidden away in there!

Stock Up!

Boosting your inventory stocks early on can still be done while tucked inside your shelter. As long as you've first stocked

up on materials such as wood, cobblestone, coal, and raw iron, you can keep busy getting loaded up and ready for adventure once daylight appears again!

Iron Crafting

To smelt raw iron, place it in the top of your furnace with a fuel, such as coal, in the bottom.

Fix It!

All tools become damaged over time after use. Iron tools can be repaired with an anvil (see page 69).

Get Cooking!

You can also cook any leftover raw meat in your inventory that you've collected from killing animals during the day. This means that you will have cooked food at your disposal for whenever your energy drops the next day. If you can, craft more than one furnace, and place them on the ground inside your shelter. Multiple furnaces means quicker smelting times!

MINE THE GAP!

Go on—take the plunge and try mining underground in your shelter! It may seem frightening at first, but you won't get far unless you explore under there.

What's Down There?

In these beginner days, it makes sense to go mining under the ground from within the safety of your shelter or base—at least you know that no hostile mobs will be coming from behind you. Beware, though, as they're likely to be lurking in the layers beneath you!

See the Light

Make sure your inventory is equipped with lots of torches and tools. In fact, torches can be a good item to help you find your way out of tunnels, twists, and dark caves. As you mine and explore, place torches on blocks on one side only. Then, when you want to head back out to the surface, just make sure the torches appear on the other side. Clever, huh?

Craft a Ladder

Here's a top way to "step up" your Minecraft skills! A **ladder** is an item that will help you get back up to your shelter and down again safely once you've created a route. A ladder is crafted by using seven sticks, arranged just like this. Remember to craft some ladders before you head underground, since you may not have your crafting table with you once you're down in the deep!

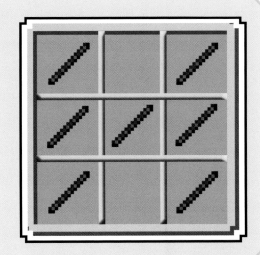

Underwater

Water will still feature frequently while under the surface, especially around lava and obsidian. You could mine clay blocks under the water, but it's tricky because you mine five times slower when your top half is under the water. Plus, your air supply soon runs out! When doors and fence blocks are placed under the water, they create a helpful air pocket.

EXTRA UNDERGROUND
PROTECTION!

Check out these quick and easy instructions to keep you safe and well below the surface . . .

Trapdoor

Want a secret entrance to your underground mine and increased protection from mobs? Place a **trapdoor**

block over the entrance, and you're done. Wooden trapdoors are crafted with six planks arranged in two rows of three.

Dark Caverns

Be on the lookout for **caves**, also known as caverns, which are natural structures. They are dark and will attract scary mobs. But they will also be a place to mine great ores such as coal, iron, and even diamond, depending on the biome you're in.

Hanging a Lantern

Hanging a **lantern** is another way to light up an area underground and keep those creepy mobs away. Lanterns are more decorative than torches, too. The crafting recipe is more complicated, with eight iron nuggets (smelted iron tools or weapons) and a torch placed in the middle.

Stair Blocks

Stair blocks were mentioned on page 57, but here you can use them for their correct purpose. Placing stairs when you're underground is a smart way to climb out again because they reduce your hunger levels much less than jumping does.

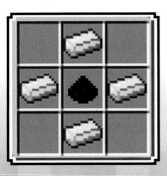

Do You Have the Time?

When you're underground, you have no idea of what time it is. Craft a clock using four gold ingots (smelted gold ore) and redstone dust (collected from redstone ore) like this.

Frame It!

Then, craft an item frame with this recipe of eight sticks and leather. Leather is dropped by defeated cows, mooshrooms, donkeys, horses, mules, hoglins, and llamas. Place the item frame on a wall, then the clock inside it—this frees the clock from using a spot in your hotbar.

STEP 4—
KEEP CRAFTING

Crafting is the way that you make items and blocks in
Minecraft. You've already been crafting quite a bit so far,
creating things like the all-important crafting table, tools,
doors, fences, and torches. This next section delves deeper
into the cool crafting world to reveal more pointers on
progressing your crafting skills even further to help you
advance in the game.

RECIPE BOOK

The recipe book is a handy way to get to know some important Survival crafting recipes.

Check Your Book

Click on the green book icon to open the recipe book panel. So that you don't have to remember gazillions of crafting recipes from the game, players can search through to see what's what in the book. Searching can be done by category, including construction, equipment, items, and nature, or by typing in a particular thing.

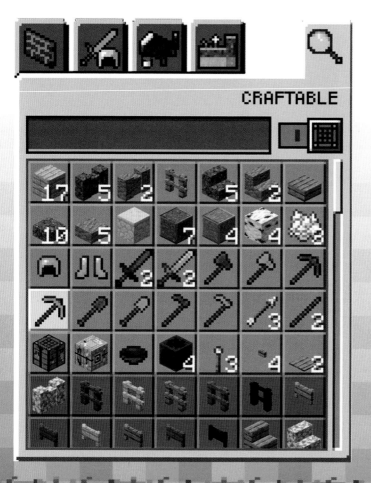

Handy Helper

Obviously, the recipe book doesn't let you craft a recipe if you don't have the resources. If something appears in a red box, this means that you do not possess all of the required ingredients. The recipe book speeds up your crafting, which is a great help for when you mine farther afield and have the added pressure of fending off attackers.

All Outcomes

The recipe book system covers all outcomes, from weapons and tools to armor, dyes, carpets, boats, and scaffolding. Cleverly, some recipes become available to you if you mine just one of its components. For example, if you collect redstone dust by mining redstone, the compass recipe is available, while the fishing rod recipe is revealed once string is in your inventory.

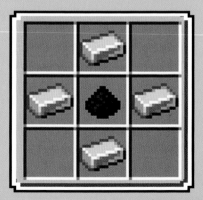

Cutting Edge

The stonecutter is an alternative to the crafting table, which can be used for most types of stone. It enables stone items to be crafted in smaller amounts and, in some cases, outputs more items for the quantity of stone you put in.

REPAIR JOB

Over time and with use, most tools, weapons, and items lose durability and become less effective. These crafting techniques let you repair them with ease!

Durability

The durability of something can be seen by the small green bar underneath it. If it's full of green, that's great, but if it's well below half, then it's lacking in durability and needs to be looked at! Wood objects wear out super fast, stone ones a bit slower, and iron much slower.

Repair It!

Either the 2x2 crafting grid or the 3x3 crafting table can be used to repair. You'll need to place two of the items (of the same type and material) that need repairing in the grid, to be rewarded with one new and improved item in the output slot. This can be much quicker than collecting everything you need to make a new item.

Grab an Anvil

Using an anvil also repairs items, and they will keep any enchantments they have as well. This is the crafting recipe for the anvil repair method, which uses three iron blocks and four iron ingots. The same as with the crafting table repair method, two items with partial durability can be placed in the anvil to produce a single repaired item.

More Than One Benefit

The anvil can also take the partial durability item that needs fixing, plus a material needed to originally create it, to make the repair. So, for example, a gold ingot can be placed in it to repair a gold sword.

DID YOU KNOW?

Anvils can be used to rename an item as you repair it.

15 QUICK
CRAFTING TIPS!

Check out these helpful quick crafting tips to get your creative game up with the best!

1

Get in Shape

Most items must be crafted in the correct recipe order, meaning that ingredients must line up in a certain way in your crafting table. These are called shaped recipes. Shapeless recipes can be arranged in any way, though, and these include some scary items!

2

Time for Bed

If you're lucky enough to locate a busy village, then there could be a bed in it for you to sleep in. This will keep you from having to craft your own. When you do craft your own bed, you can later change the color by using a colored dye in a crafting recipe.

3

Sweet Stuff

Sugar cane is a cool crafting item. Found near water, especially in the desert biome, it's a crafting ingredient for paper (essential in crafting books) and in producing regular sugar. Sugar is then used in crafting cakes and potions and for healing horses.

4

Bale Out

Commonly scattered in villages and plains, and sometimes cropping up in dry desert and savanna biomes, hay bales reduce fall damage by 80 percent. You can craft a hay bale with nine wheat and then use it to breed llamas, feed horses, and make a signal fire.

5

Knock, Knock

Simple wooden doors are crafted by placing six wooden planks in your crafting table. This will then craft three doors. If you only need a single door, the spare doors can be used as helpful fuel in a furnace.

6 Super Smoker

A smoker is a type of furnace that cooks food much, much faster. It can be crafted using four logs and a furnace, and it means that you can get plenty of cooked food stored quickly into your inventory.

7

Blast Off

The best way to smelt ore blocks, tools, and armor made of iron and gold is to use a blast furnace. The recipe needs five iron ingots, three smooth stone (smelted regular stone), and a furnace.

8 Clever Crafting

Be careful not to craft too many items and blocks, since you may not use them, and it will be a waste of time and precious resources. With experience, you will begin to sense how many things you should craft from the start. Often, having a good store of wood and ores is the best first step.

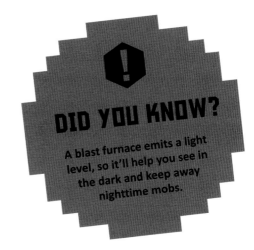

DID YOU KNOW?

A blast furnace emits a light level, so it'll help you see in the dark and keep away nighttime mobs.

9 Fab Slabs

Heard of slabs? They are half the size of their regular blocks, and six of them can be easily crafted by placing three matching full-size blocks, such as planks, stone, and bricks, into a recipe. Slabs can be used for steps, roofs, stands, barrels, composters, and daylight detectors.

10

Wonder Wall

Like fences, walls are good for keeping mobs away from shelters but are much more decorative. They are crafted in a stack of six using six blocks of stuff like granite, cobblestone, or mossy cobblestone, then placed easily in the location where you want them.

11 Store More

This is such a simple step, but crafting a chest is easy (use eight planks of any wood), and they give you extra storage space for items. When items are stored in your chest, they are then removed from your inventory to free up valuable space. Store stuff here that perhaps you don't currently need—you can always retrieve and use it later on.

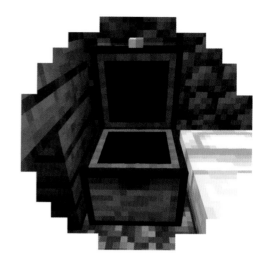

12

Water Ways

If you're moving around a new area and want to cover ground and explore quickly, remember that a boat on water moves faster than you walking over ground. Just arrange five planks in your crafting table, and add a wooden shovel to the center of their recipe. Happy rowing!

13

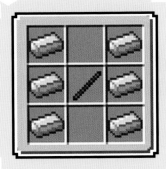

Rail Ready

Rails create a track for minecarts to travel on, moving blocks around your world. They are crafted with iron ingots and a stick, like this. Most peaceful and neutral mobs won't go across them, so it can create a handy type of animal pen!

14

Sign Here

Don't get lost or forget vital instructions when you are exploring your world, whether that's above or below the surface. Craft a sign using any six matching wood planks and a stick, and place it exactly where you need to display some info. You can also edit a message onto the sign. Very helpful!

15

Bright Idea

A jack o'lantern is a block that gives off a light source of 15 . . . plus, they look ultra cool! For a fun way to create light, craft one by using a carved pumpkin (created from a normal pumpkin fruit block being hit with shears) placed in a recipe with a torch. Jack o'lanterns can be used to build snow and iron golems.

STEP 5— GET MINING

Mining is all about collecting the things you need in Minecraft, from ore blocks to wood, stone, food, and naturally generated items that may appear in places like villages and abandoned mineshafts. This section gives you more mining tips, and reveals how a spot of helpful trading can really stock up your inventory.

AWESOME ORES

Precious and often rare, ores are mined below the surface of the ground and are vital in crafting objects that do specific jobs. Dive down into more ore-some details!

Redstone Ore

An extremely useful and popular ore, redstone generates in the Overworld between layers 0 to 15—just look for the distinctive red speckles. It's a smelting ingredient in redstone dust, which is used to craft items like the redstone lamp, redstone torch, and a dropper. You need an iron pickaxe or higher to mine it—and watch out for lethal lava nearby!

DID YOU KNOW?

At first, diamond ores were called emerald ores and emerald ores were ruby ores.

Power Play

Redstone dust is needed to make redstone power, which can be thought of as like an electric circuit that powers blocks. Objects such as a door, rail, or an explosive TNT block can be operated by the power of redstone dust.

Emerald Ore

You need to head up to the extreme hills and mountains to track down this rare ore. Found in single blocks with a pretty green pattern, it drops one emerald ore per block after being mined with an iron or diamond pickaxe or better. If you want to do some trading with villages, then you'll need this pretty and precious ore!

Diamond Ore

Appearing in most biomes from levels 0 to 15, diamond is a gorgeous ore, with one diamond dropping from each ore block mined. Diamonds are required to craft the toughest weapons, tools, and armor, plus enchantment tables and jukeboxes.

Lapis Lazuli Ore

This fancy-named ore is part of the enchantment process (see page 164 onward). Discovered between levels 0 to 30, with more common traces between 11 and 27, just look for bright blue fragments among the gray. A stone pickaxe or better will do the job to deliver this delightful ore into your inventory.

Gold Ore

The good news is that gold ore exists in pretty much all biomes, but it's still a very rare material. Look for it at levels 31 or lower. Mined with an iron pickaxe or better, it drops raw gold which can be smelted to produce gold ingots and crafted to produce powered rails, golden tools, and weapons or the golden apple.

DID YOU KNOW?

Lapis lazuli also works as a color dye ingredient.

Obsidian

Although it's not an ore, obsidian is still found under the surface like ores, and it forms when water hits against orange lava. Mined only using a diamond pickaxe, it's difficult to discover early in game. It takes around 10 seconds to mine each obsidian block—so you need to put the time in for this one! Obsidian is the hardest block that can be mined in the game, as the base layer of bedrock can't be broken. The block is part of building a Nether portal and used in the enchantment table process.

MORE MINING MATTERS

Get to know what a silk touch tool does, why you should listen carefully when mining, and plenty of other wise things to do while you're collecting resources!

Silk Touch

Mining ores, such as diamond ore, emerald ore, lapis lazuli ore, and blocks such as glass, with a silk touch tool gives you certain benefits. It's a type of enchantment and can be added to a pickaxe, axe, shovel, and shears. Silk touch lets you mine a block itself instead of the drop it makes. So, mine diamond ore with a silk touch pickaxe to get the diamond ore block and not a dropped diamond in your inventory. The benefit of this is that you can then use a tool with a fortune enchantment to mine those blocks, in the hope that it drops more good stuff!

Adding Silk Touch

Silk Touch is also the only way to mine glass and ice without breaking it into lots of pieces. It can also be used to turn ice into water. Silk touch is added through the enchanting table or the anvil (see pages 172—173).

Listen Carefully

As well as keeping your hands busy, keep your ears tuned when you are mining, too! There is a chance you'll hear lethal lava boiling, water running, groans, and all kinds of things. You'll take a risk if you head toward these sounds.

DID YOU KNOW?

Water buckets are useful if you come into direct contact with lava. Ouch!

Get Some Rest

When you're spending a lot of time mining underground, remember to set up a bed and sleep in it. This makes sure your spawn point is set at this point if you're unlucky and die. Placing items in a chest means that they won't be lost if you're wiped out and forced to respawn.

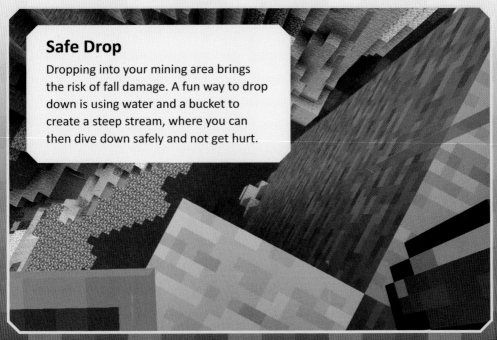

Safe Drop

Dropping into your mining area brings the risk of fall damage. A fun way to drop down is using water and a bucket to create a steep stream, where you can then dive down safely and not get hurt.

Subtitles

In Java Edition, players can turn on subtitles found in the settings area. This helps you to be aware of any nasty sounds creeping up on you (such as unfriendly footsteps!) by reading the onscreen caption.

Water Bucket

Another way that a water bucket can be helpful is when you place the water on lava, turning it into obsidian. Place the water back in the bucket, then mine the awesome obsidian!

Branch Mining

Branch mining is a technique where you create a long underground tunnel, with uniform tunnels coming off it that lead back to the main tunnel in a tight U-shape. This helps keep you from getting lost, sees you scoop up lots of blocks, and gives you great sight of any approaching mobs. Ace tactics!

Block It Off

To keep yourself from getting lost in some of your homemade shafts and mines, you may want to block them up once you've come out of them and have returned to your main tunnel or space. This acts as a reminder that you don't need to visit that area again— especially if you place unusual or colored blocks in the way.

Tasty Tip

Fishing while it's raining increases your chance of catching fish and amazing items to build up your food supply. The fishing rod recipe uses three sticks and two string.

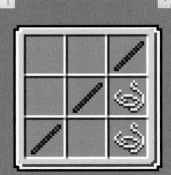

TRADING TIPS

As well as mining for helpful items, you can also trade with villagers to pick up the precious objects that will keep you going in Minecraft Survival.

What Is Trading?

Villagers, apart from nitwits, babies, and the unemployed, can trade with players. They will either want your emeralds for their items or offer up emeralds for your items. It's a much safer way of getting good stuff in your inventory without having to do risky mining.

What Types of Traders Are There?

Village traders start at novice, then apprentice, journeyman, expert, and master. Each experience level wears a different badge. Villagers have experience and can level up to move to a higher mark. You will also get XP after trading.

DID YOU KNOW?

A player with a Hero of the Village status effect gets a trading discount. This effect is achieved by defeating a raid, made up of waves of mob attacks caused by a player having a bad omen effect after defeating a patrol leader in a pillager outpost.

What Do Traders Offer?

This varies depending on what job they do. There are 13 professions, ranging from weaponsmith and toolsmith to butcher, cartographer, and leatherworker. Interact with a villager to find out what they offer and for what price. A novice level fisherman, for example, may trade 20 string for one emerald.

What Should You Collect?

Whatever you need! If it's weapons that you want, then look for the weaponsmith. If you're low on armor, then start trading with the armorer for equipment to protect you in combat. If you have a lot of a certain item, you may be able to trade it with a villager for emeralds to help your future deals. Good luck!

STEP 6— BUILD BETTER SHELTERS

A shelter, base, or house . . . whatever you like to call it, this building is very important in your world. It's the place where you keep safe from enemies and store items, plus the starting point for each day before you farm and trade in daylight. After several days, be brave enough to improve your shelter, and begin to build a better structure. Be proud of what you create, and make it look nice and work well!

HOME WORK

Want some awesome advice on upgrading your Survival shelter? Then you've come to the right place!

Win with Windows

Adding windows is a great tip. You can then see who's outside, whether that's villagers or mobs, and if it's night or day. Thinner glass panes are better than glass blocks, plus they look much neater. Panes can be mined with a silk touch tool or crafted with this recipe. Six glass blocks make 16 panes (glass blocks are crafted by smelting sand or red sand).

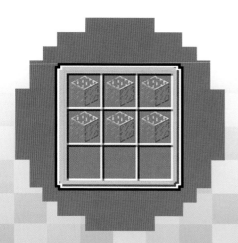

Floor Plans

Use slabs (half-size regular blocks) of materials like wood and stone to create a nice floor space. Using slabs is much better than having to dig out your ground and then place blocks—what a waste of time and resources that is!

Auto Doors

Make a quick auto-opening inside door device by placing a wooden or stone pressure plate against it. Crafted by simply placing two stone or planks next to each other in your crafting grid, it soon adds a hi-tech touch to your shelter.

DID YOU KNOW?

If you're inside an igloo, check under the carpet for a trapdoor leading to a basement. Around 50 percent of igloos have them.

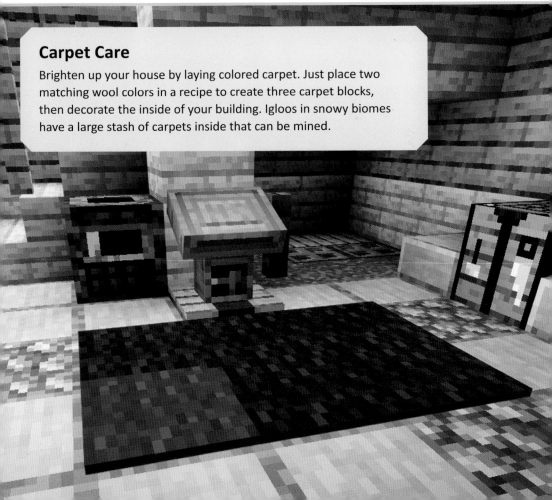

Carpet Care

Brighten up your house by laying colored carpet. Just place two matching wool colors in a recipe to create three carpet blocks, then decorate the inside of your building. Igloos in snowy biomes have a large stash of carpets inside that can be mined.

SHELTER SELECTION

There are all kinds of shelters and houses you can build in the Overworld. Flick through these for some ideas to get you busy with your blocks!

Village House

Okay, so this isn't one that you need to build from scratch, but it's a perfectly good idea to take over an existing village house and claim it as your own.

GOOD FOR . . .
customizing. Add a second floor to increase your space, and design specific rooms, such as a storage room to house chests.

Tower

Build an imposing tower to impress everyone (well, just the villagers and mobs!). You don't need a great deal of land space—just make sure you're not scared of heights!

GOOD FOR . . . views around the landscape. Take a peek around before you venture out, to check that enemies are not lurking. Towers are also easy to see and keep you from getting lost.

Underground Bunker

With at least two entrances/exits, you can make a quick retreat to, and escape from, an underground bunker. Adding furniture makes it feel more "above the surface" cozy and homelike.

GOOD FOR . . . resources. You don't need a lot of materials; just a strong pickaxe and a shovel will get you started.

Skyscraper

Maybe this doesn't need to reach the clouds literally, but a huge high-rise building (taller than a tower) is a grand statement of a house. Extravagant, but impressive!

GOOD FOR . . . storage, viewing, and showing off! Great protection from attacks, with plenty of open spaces so you can aim down at the ground.

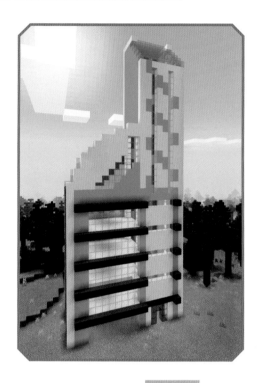

Tree House

Set high in the tree canopy of many biomes, you can even spread it out to other trees to boost space and attractiveness. Make sure there's a ladder handy!

GOOD FOR . . . sniping enemies and keeping mobs at bay, except pesky spiders.

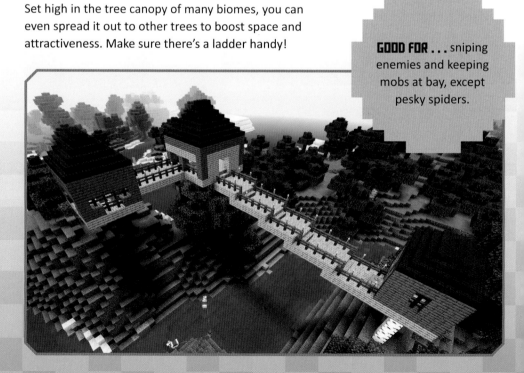

Cottage

Cottages are pretty to look at and carry a traditional homelike vibe. On the inside, this is a home that can also be built for protection and storage, with rooms for crafting.

GOOD FOR . . . blending in with a village. Perhaps the zombies and creepers will think a sweet old person lives there, not a master Minecrafter like you!

Skeleton Frame

Don't be afraid to build something using just pillars and horizontal frames at first, so that you can step back and check that you're happy before filling it in with solid walls, roofs, and so on.

GOOD FOR . . . Getting the building results you want. It's awful to spend time creating, then not like what you've done. This step-by-step approach really works.

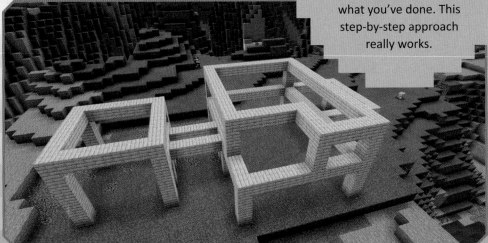

INTERESTING INTERIORS

Interiors in Survival are usually less elaborate than in Creative—but there are still some important things to keep in mind.

Safe Storage

One of the main things you'll want is storage. Chests used to be the only way of doing this, but the introduction of barrels has changed things. Barrels open at the front, which means they can be stacked and built into walls. This makes them more space-efficient than chests, and a barrel can contain the same quantities as a chest, with 27 item slots. The only disadvantage they have is that, unlike chests, they don't combine when two are placed next to each other.

Let There Be Light

Lighting not only helps you see but also prevents mobs from spawning. Lighting options in Minecraft used to be limited to torches, but now a lantern can be crafted from a torch plus eight iron nuggets and gives out a light level of 15 compared with a torch's level of 14. Soul lanterns can also be crafted by using a soul torch. Sea lanterns can be crafted from prismarine or found in ocean monuments or sea ruins—but must be mined with a tool enchanted with Silk Touch. Candles can be crafted from string and honeycomb, and a cluster of four gives out a light level of 12.

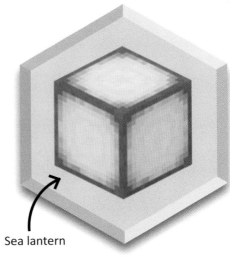

Sea lantern

Frog's Dinner

When a small magma cube is consumed by a frog, it drops a froglight. There are three different colors of froglight: frogs from warm environments give pearlescent froglights, temperate frogs produce ochre froglights, and cold frogs give verdant froglights.

STEP 7—FARM FOR RESOURCES

In Survival, farming can involve growing your own crops and edible items to keep your inventory packed with helpful foods. It also involves farming animals for your own benefit, which is fun and gives a great sense of achievement in the game. You may not be familiar with what it takes to become a successful farmer, but take a look through these pages, and you soon will be!

10 TOP
FARMING TIPS!

Here's a quick flick through some essential farming dos and don'ts to get you started out in the fields!

1

Wonderful Water

Water is essential in crop farming. The best growers give their plants no more than four blocks of water, so that crops grow to their best ability. You could also dig a water trench and use a bucket to fill it with water to create a water source.

2

Fab Farmland

Farmland is the block from which seeds and root vegetables grow. It's created by using a hoe tool (recipe shown here) to till dirt or grass blocks, or you could plant in existing farmland. Light is also vital for crop growth, with a level of nine or better in the block above the crop. Torches boost nighttime growing.

3

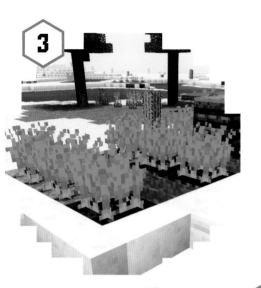

Plant Power

Destroy tall grass so that you can collect wheat seeds to plant in your farmland. Beet seeds are often discovered in abandoned mineshaft, dungeon, and woodland mansion chests. Carrots and potato crops can be mined from villages and then planted in your field to grow more.

DID YOU KNOW?

You can even grow crops underground or indoors if the light level allows it.

4

Happy Meal

Most plants take two to three days to fully grow and reach the stage of being harvested with any tool. Add bone meal as a fertilizer to really speed up the growing. Bone meal's crafted from placing a bone (dropped by a defeated skeleton) into a recipe.

5

Tasty Fruit

Farmland will also grow pumpkins and melons. Melon seeds can be collected from melons in jungle biomes, with pumpkins popping up in lots of grassy biomes. Both grow in a similar way to other crops—but they need space around them to develop before harvesting.

6

Tool Tactic

Harvesting plants can be done with any type of tool, from wood to diamond! They won't get damaged, so you can mine crops with a tool that's low in durability and it won't make any difference.

7

Keep Out

You don't want rabbits chewing on your carrot crops or creepers trampling all over your hard-earned vegetables before you've harvested them! Place a wooden fence around your farmland for protection. It looks very stylish and helps divide your land. You could have fenced-off farms for particular crops.

8

Light Up

Light is important, but you don't want to waste growing space. Float blocks above your rows of crops, and place torches on each side to maximize the use of your farmland. Torches can also be placed on fence posts.

9

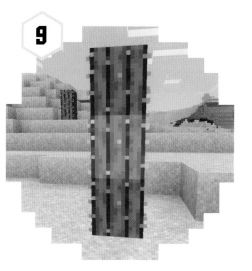

Wide Range

Other types of vegetation that can be farmed include tree saplings and cactus blocks—but don't try to eat these because they won't be very nice on your taste buds!

10

Hop to It

A hopper block can be used in the farming process to store crops in a chest. Five iron ingots and a chest are needed to craft a hopper, then it can be placed above or to the side of a chest. Put crops in the hopper to store it directly into the chest—keep a food chest in your base.

DID YOU KNOW?

Place a crafted sign with edited text in the ground to remind you of what you're growing in an area.

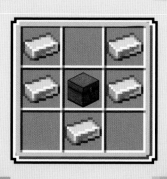

ANIMAL FARMING

Keep your belly full by keeping a bunch of helpful farm animals close by. Here's some guidance on getting the most from your animals.

Farm animals such as pigs and cows can be killed and their collected meat used for food, either raw or cooked. Of course, if that keeps happening, the animals will disappear, and you'll have no meat to scarf down when you're hungry!

Fence Your Animals

Breeding animals makes sure that you keep their numbers up. Build a secure area on flat land using fences and a gate to keep certain animals together. It can be tricky to lead an animal into your pen—hold out the food they need to breed, and they should follow you. You need two of a particular animal for them to breed and produce a baby.

Baby Animals

Feeding the animals while they are eight blocks or closer to each other will put them into love mode. A baby should soon appear and then take about 20 minutes to reach adulthood. Killing a baby animal does not drop any meat or experience.

Not Too Close

Animals need to be fenced in and close enough for them to breed, but if they are too close, they could get out through the barrier panels. Turn the page for a closer look at some farmyard creatures.

DID YOU KNOW?

Animals usually need light levels of seven or higher to spawn, so keep farms and pens well lit.

Pigs

Grassy areas attract these oinking creatures, and they can also spawn around butcher houses in villages. Getting a mouthful of beets, carrots, or potatoes can see a pair breed and create a cute piglet. Raw pork chop restores three hunger, and cooked pork is rated at eight.

GOOD FOR . . . riding! You can put a saddle on a pig and ride around—it doesn't achieve anything, but it is fun!

Cows

Wheat is the magic ingredient needed to feed cows so that a pair will breed. Cows drop leather and raw beef and can be milked. As with all breeding animals, you can take them to a pen using a leash (crafted with four string and a slimeball dropped by a slime mob).

GOOD FOR . . . milk. Keep a bucket with you to milk a cow, and use it to remove a poison effect.

Chickens

Raw chicken meat rewards you with two hunger, but cook it and this increases to six. Yum! Eggs are dropped by adult chickens every 10 minutes or so, which can then be used to craft cakes and pumpkin pies. Eggs can also be thrown at mobs to knock them back, and this may also spawn a baby chicken.

GOOD FOR . . . feathers. After being killed, chickens can drop one or two feathers, which can be used to craft an arrow.

Rabbits

Our hopping friends are pretty rare, but they can be bred if fed dandelions and carrots (this includes golden carrots, too!). Rabbit hide leather and meat are dropped if they are defeated. Remember that leatherworker villages are interested in the leather in a trade.

GOOD FOR . . . looking cute in your world! Beware of fox predators.

Sheep

Like cows and chickens, sheep also drop a helpful item while they're alive. When sheared, they produce one to three wool for use in recipes such as bed and carpets, and the wool regrows after eating grass. Feed a pair wheat to make them breed.

GOOD FOR ...
dyeing different colors!
Baby sheep can appear
in a variety of wool colors
and there's even
a super-rare chance
you'll get a pink one!

Llama

Introduced in 2016, llamas can be bred and farmed for their leather, but they're useful for carrying stuff once equipped with a chest. Leading a llama will see others join in to form a lovely llama caravan!

GOOD FOR ...
standing out! Llamas
can be equipped with
bright carpets to help
tell them apart.

Mooshroom

A mooshroom is a weird-looking type of cow that's only located in the mushroom island biome. If you don't believe it's related to the cow, just shear one to see it drop five mushrooms and change into a cow. Strange times!

GOOD FOR . . .
making mushroom stew. Milk it with a bowl to create the tasty food.

STEP 8— STAY FED

You don't want black drumsticks filling up your hunger bar—it's a sure sign that Steve or Alex are in deep trouble! Keeping well fed is fundamental in Minecraft, so that means knowing all about farming, food, and eating as you explore and battle. The next six pages spill the beans on some clever cuisine tips to keep your appetite from getting in the way of your adventures!

MASTER THE MENU!

Time to take in these hints and guides to getting the most from what's on the Minecraft menu. Dive in and enjoy the tasty advice!

1

Breadwinner

Bread may seem like a boring and dull food, but it's useful to loot from village, dungeon, and woodland mansion chests. It's crafted using just three wheat and will replenish five food hunger points. Having a good stack of food is sensible and easy to achieve.

2

Bread for Breeding

Sticking with the bread theme . . . it's more difficult to make villagers breed compared to animals, but the "food of love" can help you! Throw three bread to a village pair, and it will help make them more willing to breed, which will then keep your village busy and productive.

3

Fishing Forever

Fishing (see page 85) can be done in any amount of water, and unlike farm animals, fish will never run out! It can take awhile to get what you want from the water, such as salmon and cod, but it's easy and there's no risk involved. Don't eat everything you catch, though—the pufferfish will have a negative impact on you!

DID YOU KNOW?

Casting a fishing rod can also help you test and trigger a pressure plate from a safe distance away.

4

Cookie Time

Who doesn't like a sweet treat after a hard day of crafting and mining? Thanks to cocoa beans, which can be found around trees in jungle biomes, they can be added to a recipe with two wheat to make a tasty batch of eight cookies. They only restore two hunger, but are totally delish!

5

Pumpkin Party

Gamers love chomping on a big piece of pumpkin pie! Helpfully, it can be crafted using only a crafting grid and not a table. It requires the ingredients of sugar, egg, and pumpkin. This baked good restores an epic eight hunger and should be kept in your inventory for a big boost, as you progress and journey through your world.

DID YOU KNOW?

Use a carrot on a stick to lead pigs into your farming pen.

6

Golden Greats

Don't miss the chance to gobble up a golden apple and a golden carrot! Golden apples can be crafted with nine gold ingots and an apple, or sometimes they're discovered in chests. They restore four hunger and also give you absorption and regeneration effects. Golden carrots give you six hunger and also help in breeding, taming, and healing horses.

7 Crazy Carrot

Earlier, you read that you can saddle a pig and ride it, which is pretty pointless, to be honest! If you place a fishing rod and carrot in a recipe, the carrot on stick item can then be used to boost and control the pig while riding it. Perhaps not the best use of the vegetable, but worth trying!

8

Make Cake

Cake is a resource-heavy recipe, requiring three milk buckets, three wheat, two sugar, and one egg, but the hard work is worth it. A cake has seven slices, with each worth two hunger for a max restoring of 14 points! Remember that cake needs to be placed before being used, and even a silk touch tool can't re-collect it.

9

Clever Cooking

You know cooked meat rewards you better than raw stuff, but powering up a furnace or smoker should be done wisely. Coal, for example, can cook more than one item at a time, so have several things ready to roast, so that fuel isn't wasted and your inventory gets full quicker.

DID YOU KNOW?

A campfire block can also be used to cook food.

10

Hi, Honey!

Get your lips around a sweet honey bottle item! This delicious drink has the power to replenish six hunger and is crafted from four glass bottles and a honey block. Plus, honey bottles are effective in removing a poison effect on a player. It is sweet stuff, indeed!

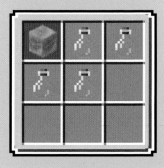

11

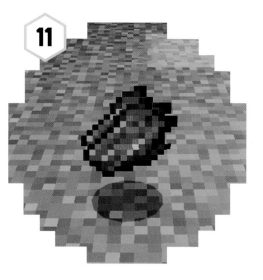

Frightening Flesh

Rotten flesh is dropped by defeated zombies, zombie villagers, zoglins, and other nasty things. It can restore four hunger, but there's also a high risk of inflicting hunger on a player instead. It's sure risky gobbling up this type of food, but in an emergency, it might be your only option!

12

Meal Maker

Remember to recycle! A composter is a smart block that lets you turn compostable items, such as apples, carrots, bread, and pumpkins, into bone meal. Bone meal can then go on crops to help them grow quickly. A composter is made with seven slabs (or three slabs and four fences in Java Edition) and needs items added to reach seven layers. It is a great way to make sure food is recycled and never wasted!

STEP 9— WATCH OUT FOR WILDLIFE

From iron golems and snow golems to endermen, bees, and pandas, your Minecraft world is jam-packed with creatures and characters to interact with. Some of them are always friendly and helpful, but others have changeable temperaments and can attack if provoked or under certain conditions! It's a chaotic time getting to know mobs, so sit back and learn about some of the most interesting ones . . .

FRIENDLY FACES?

You can usually rely on the following mobs to help you in your world, although some can unleash a nasty surprise . . .

Villager

This is the ultimate friendly Minecraft face and appears all over the world, from villages (obviously!) to deserts, savannas, and snowy locations. Villagers are simple folk who enjoy farming, sleeping, and a spot of trading.

APPEARANCE: This changes depending on their job, but thankfully, they look more like you than an angry monster.

ATTITUDE: Well behaved, obedient, helpful, and capable of breeding under the right conditions.

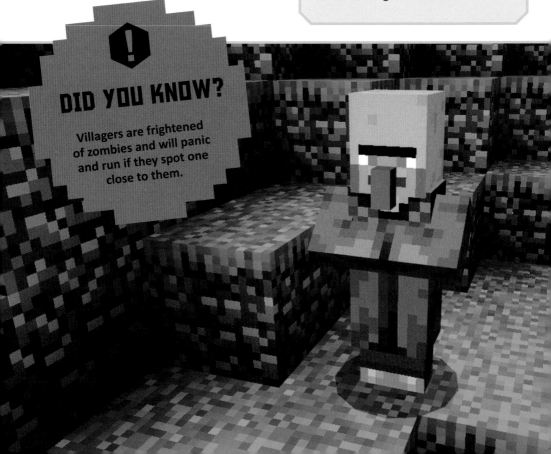

! DID YOU KNOW?

Villagers are frightened of zombies and will panic and run if they spot one close to them.

Enderman

Able to spawn in all three dimensions, this big beast is neutral at first, but will strike you down if you dare look it in the eyes! Endermen drop ender pearls, which aid teleporting and finding End portals.

APPEARANCE: Tall, gangly, creepy . . . they scare most Minecrafters!

ATTITUDE: Laid back—unless you make them angry, of course! They can teleport, too.

Polar Bear

You may get a frosty reception from this neutral mob, especially if you attack its lovable cubs—all adult polar bears within a 41x21x41 range will turn against you if you do! Polar bears don't breed, and they may drop fish if defeated.

APPEARANCE: White and cute, and the little 'uns are supersweet, too!

ATTITUDE: They'll attack by standing on their huge rear legs, but treat them well, and you won't see that terrifying sight!

Wolf

Found in packs of four around forest and taiga biomes, wolves may appear hostile, but they're only dangerous to you if you attack. They can be tamed by being fed bones and even breed if fed any meat apart from fish.

APPEARANCE: Red eyes when angered, but generally they look like a meaner, more lethal sheep!

ATTITUDE: Loyal. Tamed wolves will protect Steve or Alex against hostile mobs that attack.

Iron Golem

Powerful and protective, these neutral mobs can defend you and other villagers, and can deal damage over a wide range. They can be crafted by putting four iron blocks in a cross shape, with a jack o'lantern, pumpkin, or carved pumpkin as a head.

APPEARANCE: Long arms and a big body, iron golems have a menacing look to match their mighty powers.

ATTITUDE: Friendly folk if they're on your team, iron golems like to hand over poppies as a sign of their likable nature!

Snow Golem

Neutral mobs at first, snow golems have the job of defending against hostile mobs by throwing snowballs. Blazes (flying hostile mobs) and wolves are particularly prone to their attacking powers.

APPEARANCE: Like a snowman, to be honest! Created by two snow blocks with a pumpkin or jack o'lantern head.

ATTITUDE: Not fans of warm biomes or water, snow golems can dispense snowballs from mobs up to 10 blocks away. Plus, they look really "cool"!

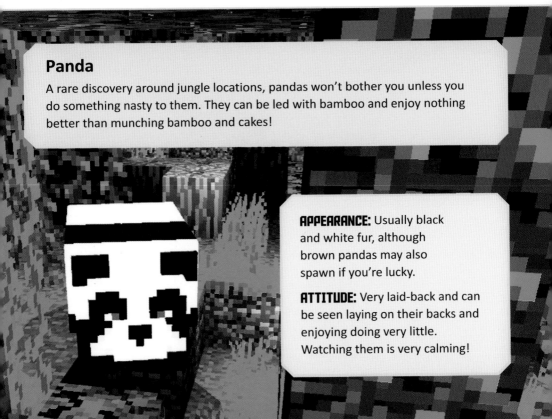

Panda

A rare discovery around jungle locations, pandas won't bother you unless you do something nasty to them. They can be led with bamboo and enjoy nothing better than munching bamboo and cakes!

APPEARANCE: Usually black and white fur, although brown pandas may also spawn if you're lucky.

ATTITUDE: Very laid-back and can be seen laying on their backs and enjoying doing very little. Watching them is very calming!

Bee

Originating in bee nests in some forest and plain biomes, bees will only get angry if they feel threatened or if their homes are attacked. They usually spawn in a group of three. Dripping honey from a hive can be collected with a honey bottle.

APPEARANCE: Buzzy and busy, they actually hover and do not fly. Bees can be led but will still attack even with a leash on.

ATTITUDE: Happy to help you, bees will follow Steve or Alex if they hold a flower and also enjoy attaching to a honey block. "Bee" nice to these guys!

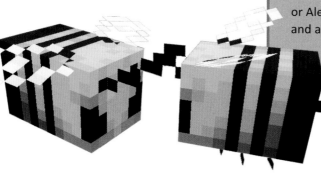

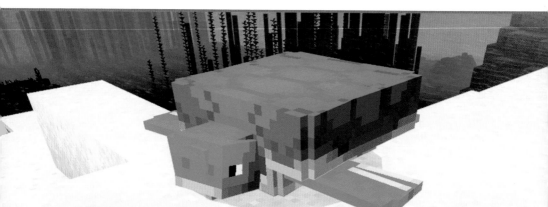

Turtle

Able to move across land and water, although much slower around the beaches they inhabit, turtles are another pretty creature that will do you no harm. Seagrass is their fave food, which will be dropped if defeated.

APPEARANCE: Green and scaly and often seen in small groups. They move speedily in water.

ATTITUDE: Fearful of predators and more comfortable in the water. A turtle never forgets the "home" beach where it hatched and returns there to lay eggs.

Parrot

Head to the jungle to spot these pretty creatures! They're rare and there's no way of breeding them, so be sure to interact with these fancy fliers if you can. Parrots can be tamed if fed seeds.

APPEARANCE: Very bright, they appear in striking shades of green, gray, cyan, red, and blue. They can often be seen on the ground if tired from flying.

ATTITUDE: Bold as brass, parrots can mimic the sound of other hostile mobs close to them, which can be very confusing!

Horse

With an ability to breed and drop leather (just like farming mobs), horses can also transport you quickly and jump over high blocks. They need to be tamed and saddled first before you can go galloping around on them. Horses will never attack you.

APPEARANCE: All kinds of colors, from gray to black, brown, and white. They look majestic as they patrol and prance around plains and savannas.

ATTITUDE: Relaxed, playful, and happy to be lead to a farm pen or ridden over open grass. When a donkey and horse breed, they make a mule.

Cat

When tamed, cats have one major benefit—creepers don't like coming near them! Cats will breed if fed raw fish and drop string if defeated. Having this lovable pet around your base can often put a smile on your face!

APPEARANCE: Black, tabby, gray, golden—cats come in a few looks depending on the parents' background. Kittens sure are some of the cutest characters in the Overworld!

ATTITUDE: Cats won't do you any harm and are helpful if a creeper comes near. They can be lazy, though, and sit around getting in your way!

! DID YOU KNOW?

Cats and ocelots will never suffer fall damage. (It's a shame Alex and Steve don't have this ability!)

Bat

These small flying mobs are not overly liked by players, but bats don't attack, and you'll know when one's around—they make a high-pitched call! Bats only come out in low light levels.

APPEARANCE: Dark, flappy, and often seen hanging around dark caves (upside down!).

ATTITUDE: Bats can be quite jumpy by nature and don't like to stay still if approached. They drop nothing when killed, so don't waste effort on them!

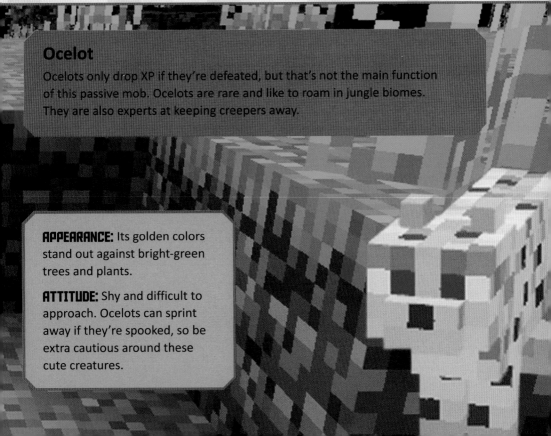

Ocelot

Ocelots only drop XP if they're defeated, but that's not the main function of this passive mob. Ocelots are rare and like to roam in jungle biomes. They are also experts at keeping creepers away.

APPEARANCE: Its golden colors stand out against bright-green trees and plants.

ATTITUDE: Shy and difficult to approach. Ocelots can sprint away if they're spooked, so be extra cautious around these cute creatures.

Spider

Spawning in several biomes and locations, spiders are neutral but become hostile if the light level is 11 or less. They can climb walls, and cave spiders are found in dungeons and abandoned mineshafts. Keep your eyes peeled for them!

APPEARANCE: Regular spiders are dark with glowing red eyes. Cave spiders are a little smaller and darker in appearance.

ATTITUDE: Both types of spiders are neutral at first, but get on the wrong side of them, and you'll need a swift attack to keep them from causing you damage.

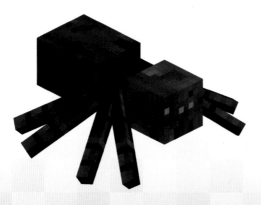

Pufferfish

Found swimming in the warm and lukewarm ocean biomes, pufferfish spawn on the surface and are classed as a passive mob. However, get close to one, and you'll soon see a big difference!

APPEARANCE: Pufferfish will puff up if a player, or most mobs, come within a five-block radius of it. It can then inflict poison damage.

ATTITUDE: Calm and unbothered, but get up close to it and there is a big difference. Don't give it cause to inflate!

DID YOU KNOW?

Wandering traders only sell items and do not buy them. This makes them different to villagers.

Wandering Trader

The mysterious wandering trader is always a welcome sight! Complete with leashed llamas, you can trade items like fish, plants, and dyes with this passive character. All trades involve emeralds.

APPEARANCE: Impressive blue clothing and a caravan of llamas means that a wandering trader is always easy to spot. They spawn randomly around the Overworld.

ATTITUDE: They stay clear of trouble and can drink invisibility potions at dusk. Llamas are ready to defend the trader if they are attacked!

Frog

Frogs spawn in swamps and also grow from tadpoles. If you come within six blocks of them while holding a slimeball, they will follow you. Feeding slimeballs to frogs enables you to breed them.

APPEARANCE: There are three variants of frog—a grayish one from warm environments, an orange one from temperate areas, and a green one from cold places.

ATTITUDE: Frogs will attack by using their tongue to pull small mobs into their mouth. They prey on slimes and small magma cubes—which drop froglights.

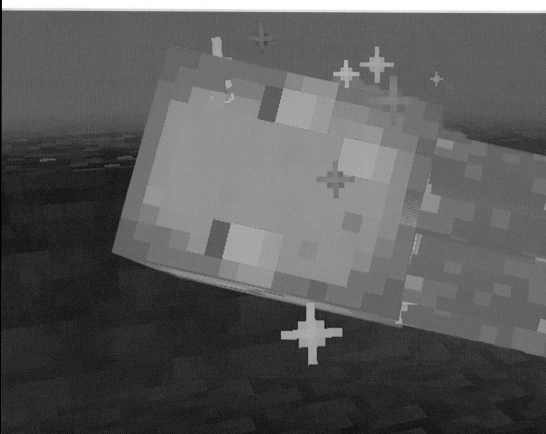

Tadpole

Tadpoles hatch from frogspawn laid by frogs, and this is the only way they spawn in the game. The type of frog they mature into depends on what biome they're in at the time.

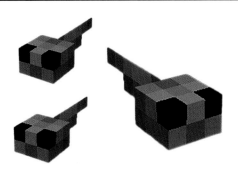

APPEARANCE: Small and dark brown, with a very thin tail.

ATTITUDE: Like frogs, tadpoles will follow a player holding a slimeball. Feeding them the slimeball will accelerate their growth into a frog. They don't survive long out of water but can be caught in a water bucket.

Glow Squid

These spawn in underwater darkness, so are most likely to be found in underground water spaces and waterlogged caves. They drop glow ink sacs when killed.

APPEARANCE: Glow squid are turquoise, and though they have a glowing appearance, they don't actually generate light.

ATTITUDE: Glow squid are passive and will swim in a chilled-out and aimless way. They can only survive for 15 seconds out of the water.

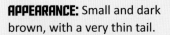

Allay

These are highly useful little creatures. If you give them an item, they will seek out any dropped versions of that same item and bring them back to you.

APPEARANCE: A bit like a blue flying fish, with fins on its sides and tail. Except it swims through the air.

ATTITUDE: An allay will follow the last player who gave it an item. They are also attracted to note blocks, and after hearing one will spend 30 seconds bringing items to that block.

Axolotl

These spawn in lush caves, in the vicinity of clay blocks. You can breed them by catching them in a water bucket, and you can also put them on a leash.

APPEARANCE: There are five different colors of axolotl—pink, brown, gold, cyan, and blue.

ATTITUDE: Axolotls will attack any aquatic mobs except dolphins, turtles, and other axolotls. They can survive on land for a short time but will die if they don't return to the water within five minutes.

Goat

Goats spawn at higher levels: snowy slopes, jagged peaks, and frozen peaks. A goat has a 2% chance of spawning as a screaming goat, which rams more frequently. And screams.

APPEARANCE: Very light, white with off-white patches, and with two gray horns on its head.

ATTITUDE: Tend to move upward if left to wander. They will jump over obstacles. They will ram anything that doesn't move, at intervals of between 30 seconds and five minutes.

Get Your Goat

Sometimes an adult goat will ram a hard block that spawns naturally where goats live, such as a tree or stone. When it does so, it drops a goat horn. There are eight different variants of goat horn, each of which makes a different sound. Normal goats drop Feel, Ponder, Seek, or Sing horns. Screaming goats drop Admire, Call, Dream, and Yearn horns. Players can use them to locate each other when exploring: they can be heard from up to 256 blocks away.

STEP 10— TAKE ON HOSTILE MOBS

One thing is for sure: These folks definitely do not want to be friends with you. Their only purpose is to attack others and defend themselves! They'll do anything to keep you away from places and keep you from progressing through the dimensions. It's time to take a deep breath and check out some of the scariest Minecraft monsters, plus what it takes to get the better of them. Stay safe out there!

KNOW YOUR ENEMIES!

There's a famous saying that you should keep your friends close, but your enemies closer. Well, perhaps not in the case of this scary selection!

Zombie

The classic Overworld mob, zombies spawn in small groups as long as the light level is below eight. They can attack players and villagers from as far as 40 blocks away and will keep attacking, even if you hit back. Noobs hate these fellas!

APPEARANCE: Green and terrifying—although husks (desert zombies) are dark brown.

ATTITUDE: Bad—they just want to get you! Baby zombies are small and speedy and can fit through 1x1 block gaps.

Drowned

Don't think you're safe from zombies in the water, either—that's where drowned mobs are lurking! They can attack at close quarters, but if they have a trident weapon, they can throw it from a distance. Totally unpleasant behavior!

APPEARANCE: Darker than a traditional zombie and with a trident in hand, there's no mistaking one.

ATTITUDE: It stinks, basically! They can attack on land and in the water at night.

Skeleton

Similar to zombies, skeletons spawn when the light is at seven or lower. Their biggest danger is that they fire arrows when inside 15 blocks of their target. Keep plenty of distance between you and these evil characters.

APPEARANCE: Gray and spindly, the bow is their biggest identifying feature.

ATTITUDE: Very relentless—they even climb stairs to get at their target. They back away from wolves, though.

Creeper

Don't allow creepers to sneak within three blocks of you—they can then explode, and it's goodnight for you and your buildings! They are silent and stealthy, until the dreaded "hsss" sound is heard when they're upon you!

APPEARANCE: Green blocks of misery and nastiness. Their sad face only adds to their creepiness.

ATTITUDE: Explosive! Defeat them and you can pick up gunpowder for later use.

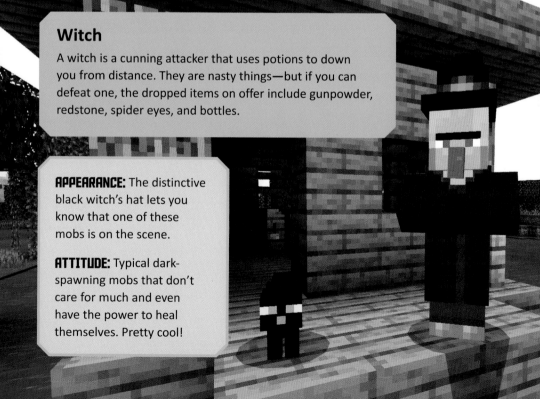

Witch

A witch is a cunning attacker that uses potions to down you from distance. They are nasty things—but if you can defeat one, the dropped items on offer include gunpowder, redstone, spider eyes, and bottles.

APPEARANCE: The distinctive black witch's hat lets you know that one of these mobs is on the scene.

ATTITUDE: Typical dark-spawning mobs that don't care for much and even have the power to heal themselves. Pretty cool!

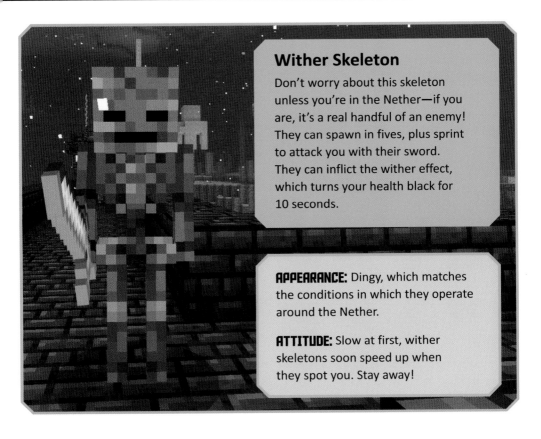

Wither Skeleton

Don't worry about this skeleton unless you're in the Nether—if you are, it's a real handful of an enemy! They can spawn in fives, plus sprint to attack you with their sword. They can inflict the wither effect, which turns your health black for 10 seconds.

APPEARANCE: Dingy, which matches the conditions in which they operate around the Nether.

ATTITUDE: Slow at first, wither skeletons soon speed up when they spot you. Stay away!

Endermite

These little monsters can spawn at the location that an enderman teleports from and even at the spot that an ender pearl lands. They do damage when up close to you, with attack strength ranging between two to three health.

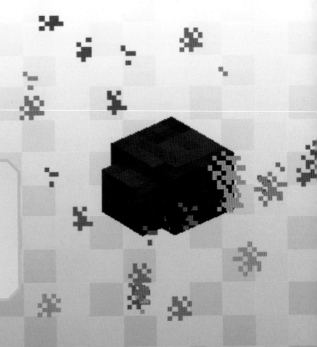

APPEARANCE: Tiny little purple terrors that pack a big punch!

ATTITUDE: They don't have a weapon, but their pesky antics can be a real headache.

Illager

Looking like a mix between a villager and a wandering trader, illagers come in two types—a vindicator and an evoker. They spawn in woodland mansions and outposts. A vindicator attacks with an axe, whereas evokers cast a spell to summon an evoker fang attack or vexes.

APPEARANCE: Evokers have longer coats, but both variants carry the look of a mob that you don't want to deal with.

ATTITUDE: The snapping fangs are an example of how evil an illager can be.

Hoglin

Hoglins spawn in the Nether's new crimson forest biome and will attack players once sighted. They are experts at hitting you with their heads and causing knockback. If they reach the Overworld or the End, they become zoglins!

APPEARANCE: Stocky and powerful, with a distinctive head and snout for charge attacks.

ATTITUDE: Spiky and very hostile, so collecting dropped meat and leather by defeating them is tough.

Vex

Look up for a group of vexes, which are flying attackers who will lunge with their sword after being summoned by an illager. They drop nothing upon defeat, which means they're no great prize in combat.

APPEARANCE: Like an illager but with flapping wings to carry them into action!

ATTITUDE: Tough little monsters who can even fly through solid blocks!

Wither

You'll see more about Nether mobs from page 198, but the wither is a boss mob that fires explosive skulls to cause complete carnage. It can even see off fire and lava attacks—the wither is a fearsome foe!

APPEARANCE: A triple-headed giant that scares the socks off just about everything!

ATTITUDE: Ferocious in its actions and appearance. You need plenty of practice and resources to come close to defeating it.

Ghast

White, hovering Nether mobs can blast fearsome fireballs once they open their evil red eyes and mouth. They are very rare and can drop gunpowder if you have the skills to shoot one down.

APPEARANCE: Big and bold with jellyfish-like tentacles that make them look super scary.

ATTITUDE: The screech they make when attacking is as frightening as their fighting skills!

Ender Dragon

This huge flying boss mob is a beast to battle with! Its 200 health makes it ultra hard to take down. It's an impressive achievement even for a player to get the chance to fight it. The ender dragon is a legendary creature.

APPEARANCE: At 16 blocks wide, it's the biggest mob in Minecraft!

ATTITUDE: With the ability to break through even obsidian, the ender dragon is a mega monster with mega power!

Learn more about the mighty Ender dragon on page 218.

STEP 11— BE A MASTER OF COMBAT

Once you know who the hostile enemy mobs are and what they can do, you need a fighting chance of beating them. Running away and hiding isn't an option, so you should know how to get the most from your weapons and learn some crucial combat tips and techniques. Be brave, be strong, and most importantly, be the best warrior you can be with your weapon drawn!

CRUCIAL COMBAT GUIDE

Flick through these fighting facts, tips and techniques for a complete guide to combat.

Melee Strikes

A melee attack happens when you are close to an opponent. This can be done with your fists, but it is much more likely to be with a sword, trident, axe, or pickaxe. Weapons used from a distance, like a bow and arrow, are called ranged weapons. Melee fighting is usually more dangerous, since you're right next to your mob target.

Critical Hit

You can deal extra damage by causing a critical hit in a melee attack—you'll see small stars appear from the target when you do. This is achieved by a player jumping, then hitting with their weapon to make contact while falling. Critical hits can also be done with a bow and arrow, as long as the weapon is fully charged (drawn back for firing).

Accuracy

Obviously, it's best to be as accurate as possible when using a weapon on a mob. Fully charging a bow, for example, increases your accuracy and hit success. Always use the crosshair target to accurately focus on the enemy in your sight. Sometimes in scrambled or panicked melee fighting, you just need to strike and hit as fast as you can, though!

DID YOU KNOW?

Knockback is also an enchantment that can be applied to a sword to boost the knockback it deals.

Knockback

As well as taking damage from a weapon attack, players and mobs can be knocked back during a fight. This causes the player to lose control very briefly—it literally knocks you back from where you were hit. In extreme cases, knockback can be fatal and cause you to fall back over a steep edge or into lava!

Escape Route

If you're really under pressure and you have an ender pearl in your inventory, you could use it as a way to escape from a combat. You'll teleport to wherever it lands, then you have a brief space of time to figure out what your next fighting move will be.

Food Fight

A clever tip is to keep a good food item (such as cooked meat) in your hotbar next to your weapon. During a fight, you could take a major hit to your health, so having food ready to gobble up quickly will get you back in a good condition and ready to continue the combat.

DID YOU KNOW?

If you can obtain elytra wings, they can be highly useful in making ranged attacks on tough-to-beat mobs!

Helping Hands

As well as using your weapons to protect yourself in battle, other items and mobs can come to your rescue. So use them wisely! Tame wolves will attack some mobs if they attack you, while creepers avoid cats. Plus, a cast fishing rod can cause knockback and reel mobs, such as guardian and elder guardian, toward you.

Safe Surroundings

In the Overworld during the day, you're basically pretty safe. No zombies, creepers, or skeletons will come for you, so you are able to relax and focus more on farming and resources, rather than on fighting and combat. Below ground in the caves or mineshafts, it's a different story, though!

SWORD

This is a legendary weapon in Survival and is usually seen as the best all-around attacking item you can have.

Iron swords are not as strong as diamond, but you'll probably use iron more since it's easier to collect and still very reliable and powerful. Swords can be effective in "hit and run" attacks, where you strike close against a mob, then move back, then move in and attack again. Repeating this deals damage and critical hits, while hopefully keeping you out of danger.

Awesome Netherite

Netherite is tougher than diamond, and it can float on lava. Netherite scraps and gold ingots can be crafted into netherite ingots, which can be used to upgrade diamond weapons and armor!

Sweep Attack

In Java, the sweep attack function allows a player a fully charged sword to strike down with the weapon and hurt mobs that are nearby. Remember that a sword can be used to break blocks, too, but at a slower rate to a pickaxe. Some mobs, such as wither skeleton and piglin in the Nether, spawn with a sword and may drop it after defeat.

Netherite Sword

A netherite sword is crafted by combining a diamond sword and a netherite ingot in a smithing table. Netherite ingots come by placing four gold ingots and four netherite scraps in a crafting grid. Smithing tables are crafted using two iron ingots and any four planks.

GOOD FOR DEFEATING: enderman, wolf, zombie, creeper.

BOW AND ARROW

Get to know the ins and outs of this cool weapon to help you strike fear around your Survival world!

Make an attack from a safe distance by using a bow equipped with arrows. They are easy to use, and a bow is crafted with three sticks and three string. Unfortunately, a bow does not come loaded with arrows, but a basic stack of four arrows is made with flint, stick, and feather. The range of an arrow shot from a bow is around 65 blocks, which is quite impressive for a weapon made from simple low-grade resources!

Take the High Ground

Arrows are affected by gravity and will fall away (arc) over distance. To combat this, aim slightly higher whenever shooting it from a long way away. Some players like to take a higher position, then shoot the arrow downward at their target.

Arrows

Bows are always wooden, but can be enhanced with enchantments. These include infinity (unlimited arrows) and flame (ignited arrows). Arrow ammunition can also be upgraded for more damage. Tipped arrows inflict a potion such as poison, harming, and weakness. In Java, a spectral arrow is crafted with four glowstone dust and a regular arrow. Plus, it will cause the glowing status effect.

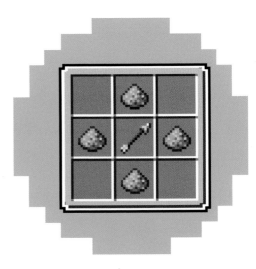

GOOD FOR DEFEATING: skeleton, skeleton horseman, and slime.

DID YOU KNOW?

An accurate arrow can trigger a wooden pressure plate and target blocks. A target block emits redstone power.

CROSSBOW

If you like the look and feel of a bow and arrow, then grab a crossbow for even more fun and success in combat situations!

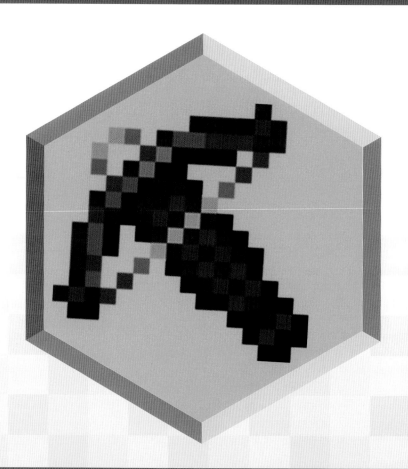

The crafting recipe for a crossbow is fairly resource heavy. It uses three sticks, one iron ingot, two string, and one tripwire hook, but the effort is worth it! You may be lucky enough to discover it in a pillager outpost chest, but whether picked up or crafted, you'll have fun shooting this awesome weapon in your world.

More Than Just a Bow

Think of a crossbow as a more powerful bow that is able to shoot arrows a little farther and with greater accuracy. On the downside, the crossbow takes longer to load compared to a regular bow, but you can keep it loaded in your hotbar for quick use.

Fully Loaded

A crossbow also needs arrows to be fully loaded or charged in order to be shot—a normal bow doesn't need to have this. When the weapon is loading, you will only be moving at creeping speed. Crossbows fire arrows in much the same way that a bow does, but they can also ping a firework rocket! This pretty ammunition deals explosion effects on your targeted mobs. Enchantments such as quick charge, multishot, and piercing can also be equipped with a crossbow.

Loot or Trade

Keep an eye out for piglins and pillagers potentially dropping this weapon. The fletcher villager is the person you want to track down if you would like to trade emeralds for items such as a crossbow, arrows, and bow.

GOOD FOR DEFEATING:
witch, illager, pillager.

AXE

That's right—the trusty and humble axe can be used
to attack! Find out how to handle it . . .

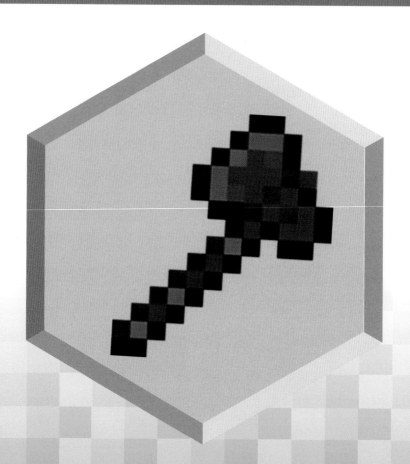

Like all weapons, there are pros and cons to using an axe in combat. First of all,
the axe is there to mine wood blocks and some plants, too! But if you're stuck for
a weapon or are in the early part of a game, equipping it from your inventory can
be very wise. A gold axe is less durable than a wooden one, and an iron, stone,
and diamond axe have an attack damage of nine.

Small but Powerful

In melee (close up) fighting, an axe can inflict heavy blows just like a sword, even though it's smaller in size. If you're playing in Java, the axe does need a little longer to recover, and it can't be used in swipe attack mode like a sword.

Shield

A shield is a very strong defense in combat, but arm yourself with an axe, and there's a chance to break through that protection. Any axe has the ability to get through a shield and disarm it for around five seconds—this could really help you to get the better of your opponent.

Drop That Axe!

The vindicator illager is a big fan of the axe, too. It uses it to deal out attacks. Take this mob down, and there's a chance of it dropping—and it may even end up being an awesome enchanted axe, too.

GOOD FOR DEFEATING: spider, zombie, zombie villager.

TRIDENT

One of the newest weapons in Survival, a trident gives you many advantages over a mob that's trying to take you down!

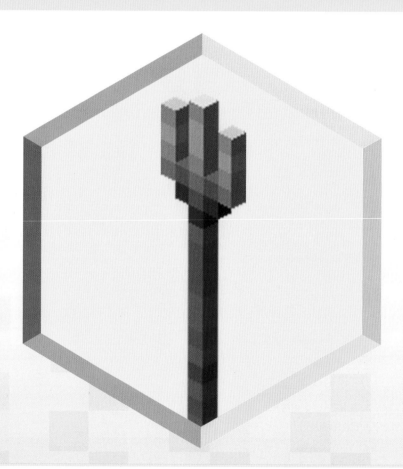

When drowned zombie mobs became part of Minecraft in 2018, it also meant the addition of the fantastic trident weapon. Rejoice! Tridents are a versatile attacking tool because they can be effective in both ranged and melee situations. Sadly for you, they can't be crafted, and your only hope is to be lucky enough to collect one that's been dropped by a defeated drowned monster. Unfortunately, that also means going up against the mob!

Keep It Charged

Scoring high in the damage stakes, a trident inflicts nine damage if landed on a mob in melee combat. Even at range, a strike will result in eight damage, so get an accurate shot in, and enemies will soon take a big hit. Interestingly, a trident's speed is not slowed when thrown in water or on land—make sure it's fully charged, by holding down the attack button until the charge bar is full, before being launched.

GOOD FOR DEFEATING: guardian, creeper, silverfish, witch.

DID YOU KNOW?

Tridents thrown by the drowned can't be picked up again by a player. But if a player throws one, it can be collected again if it lands on the ground.

MORE WEAPON TIPS!

Keep your combat and mob-bashing abilities in top shape with these extra bites of weapon-based details . . .

TNT

Obviously, the main use for an explosive TNT block is to blow mega holes in the ground and buildings above and below the surface. But if you're feeling extravagant, it can be used to wipe out mobs, too! Place it in a TNT landmine trap, and let the bad guys feel the pain!

Dispenser

This block can be used to dispense innocent and harmless items. On the flipside, it can fire out harmful stuff, such as arrows and a fire charge! A fire charge ball lights a fire wherever it lands, and it can deal as much as five damage against a mob that it strikes. Impressive results and impressive to look at!

Lava Bucket

As well as being the most efficient fuel source, when lava is placed in a bucket, it is a very handy weapon. It can be placed between you and a mob to cause a heated situation! Lava can also be placed in a dispenser.

! DID YOU KNOW?

If you're unlucky enough to be scorched by a lightning strike during a thunderstorm, you'll take five damage and hope that the rain quickly puts the blaze out!

Snowball

Hit a snow block and collect snowballs that can be thrown against mobs to create knockback. Eggs can be chucked to deal with knockback in this way, too. Blaze mobs in the Nether take three damage when struck by a snowball, and it's a cool way to cause disruption to an angry mob!

STEP 12— SOURCE YOUR ARMOR!

You won't progress far enough to brave the dangers
of the Nether and the End without knowing about and equipping
yourself with armor. In Survival, this offers a vast amount
of protection against mobs and effects, plus it can keep your
precious health bar looking good for a longer time. The following
pages reveal all the stuff you need to use and understand.

AWESOME ARMOR GUIDE

See how the armor function works, and explore the elements that go together to form this essential piece of equipment.

Armor comes in four pieces—helmet, chestplate, leggings, and boots. It is physically worn by Alex and Steve and comes in several tiers. Leather is the weakest, then there's golden, chainmail, iron, diamond—and netherite, which is the strongest.

Repair Your Armor

Armor can be damaged with use and will need repairing. The small armor bar, above health, displays how much protection it offers. Chest armor has the most protection, then leggings. Helmet and boot strength depend on the material used.

Get the Full Set

A total of 24 pieces of material are needed in order to craft a full set of armor. There are a variety of materials that can be used, depending on the armor strength desired. For example, helmets require five leather or five iron ingots, along with eight chestplates materials, seven leggings materials, and four boots materials (this totals 24).

Enchanting

You can enchant armor to give it even more magical powers! By adding enchantments, such as blast protection and depth strider (boots), you can really boost your power in combat, making you a formidable foe. Remember, only one enchantment can be applied to one piece of armor at a time.

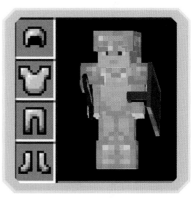

DID YOU KNOW?

Leather armor is actually more like clothing, with a helmet known as a cap and a chestplate referred to as a tunic!

THE POWER OF PROTECTION!

Fun and fascinating facts all about what armor can offer you in Survival!

Super Shield

Although it's technically not armor, a shield pretty much acts like it. Lots of players use one early in the game to defend and block both ranged and melee attacks. Placing the shield in the off-hand slot gives you an easy way to equip it. Plus, if you crouch in Bedrock, it raises the shield as protection. Shields are crafted with any six planks and an iron ingot.

DID YOU KNOW?

A charged creeper is caused by a lightning strike within four blocks of a creeper or by a trident hitting a creeper with a channeling enchantment in a thunderstorm. When one explodes, it can cause mobs to drop their head. Scary!

Mob Use

It's not only the players that can use armor—some mobs are able to stick it on, too! Zombies (including babies) and skeletons can make use of it. For example, skeletons use helmets to protect them from burning in the sun. If a defeated mob drops armor, it's a smart move to collect it!

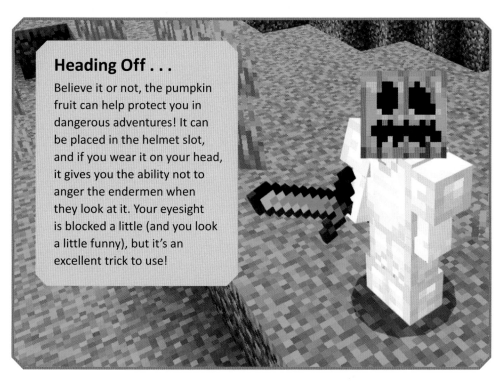

Heading Off . . .

Believe it or not, the pumpkin fruit can help protect you in dangerous adventures! It can be placed in the helmet slot, and if you wear it on your head, it gives you the ability not to anger the endermen when they look at it. Your eyesight is blocked a little (and you look a little funny), but it's an excellent trick to use!

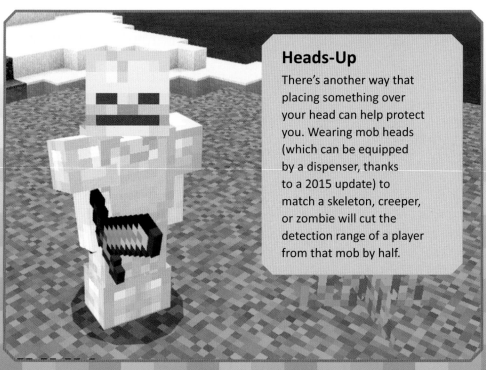

Heads-Up

There's another way that placing something over your head can help protect you. Wearing mob heads (which can be equipped by a dispenser, thanks to a 2015 update) to match a skeleton, creeper, or zombie will cut the detection range of a player from that mob by half.

Turtle-y Terrific!

Like a shield, a turtle shell is not armor, but it will bring you some protection. It's worn as a helmet and offers a player 10 extra seconds of breath while under water. On land, it can also absorb a small amount of damage. It looks funny when worn, but it does a neat job.

Make a Stand

Sometimes you don't want to stash your armor away in a chest—you might want to leave it on display. That's where the armor stand comes in! Crafted from a recipe of six sticks and a smooth stone slab, it can be used for placing your prized armor on while you decide what to wear. It's kind of a show-off item, but when you have spent time crafting your awesome armor, showing off is what you want to do with it!

Winging It

Elytra are wings found in end cities in the End. They are very important items, but be aware that they must be equipped in a player's chestplate armor slot. So, this means that a chestplate and elytra wings can't be used at the same time. Shame!

STEP 13— USE MAGIC

In need of extra help and power to boost your chances in Survival? Enchantments and potions are just what you need! Acting like special spells and effects, they can make items and players perform and react in ways that will see you master the mobs and terrain around you. Turn the page to start your journey to discovering everything there is to know about these two awesome gameplay additions!

ENCHANTMENTS

Enchantments work with items to make them more powerful. There are many ways to create them and they can do a wide range of things!

Enchantment Table

To make enchantments using an **enchantment table**, you need to have experience (XP) and lapis lazuli. This is the recipe for the enchantment table—it uses one book, two diamonds, and four obsidian. When the enchantment table is open, put the item you want to enchant (such as a weapon or armor) into the empty slot.
Three random enchantment choices will then appear. The number on the right of each enchantment shows the XP level you need to be at in order to use the enchantment. The number on the left is the number of XP and lapis lazuli you must pay for it.

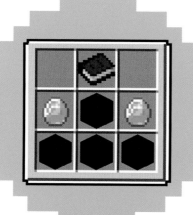

Anvil

The anvil (see page 69) can also be used to enchant something. First, you need an enchantment book. In your enchantment table, add a regular book and lapis lazuli to open up three enchantment options. Select one and apply it to the book to craft an enchanted book. Back in your anvil, the enchanted book can now be used to enchant an item with that power.

REPAIR + NAME

DIAMOND AXE

DID YOU KNOW?

When an item has been enchanted, you'll notice that it glows purple. Enchanted books can also be looted from chests and traded with villagers.

ENCHANTMENTS TO ENJOY!

Here are some of the most important, useful, and exciting enchantments that can help you get a result in your world.

Protection

When you're heading into dangerous mob situations in the Nether and Overworld, this enchantment limits the damage that your armor will take from attacks. Make this a top priority!

Mending

Unlike unbreaking, mending will repair an item that's been damaged to make it stronger again. It's classed as a treasure enchantment that needs to be found, and can't be made with an enchantment table.

Unbreaking

Going up to power level III, unbreaking is a great enchantment right through your gameplay. It works with armor, weapons, and tools to improve their durability and make them last longer.

Infinity

Instead of using up all of your arrows and needing to craft more, just apply this power, and a single arrow is enough for you to keep firing for, well . . . infinity!

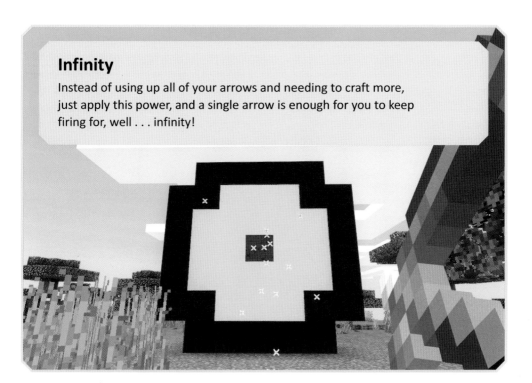

Multishot

Specifically for crossbows, this neat enchantment lets a player shoot three arrows or rockets at once, instead of the usual single shot. The arrows shoot out in a slight fan to hit a greater target.

Fire Protection

The Nether is loaded with nasty lava, so it's highly recommended to have fire protection at your fingertips! This armor enchantment reduces fire damage as well as the time that you'll spend on fire.

Fire Aspect

Another red-hot enchantment, fire aspect is an ability applied to a sword that causes a struck mob to catch fire. Sadly, Nether mobs don't suffer from burning, but it will help elsewhere in your adventures!

Looting

To increase the chance of mob drops, add the looting enchantment to your sword. Any mobs that are defeated are then more likely to drop the items that you're looking for.

Fortune

When you're mining and collecting resources, this added ability ramps up the chances of getting more drops from your mined blocks. Apply it to crops and ores to give your inventory a welcome boost of stuff.

Feather Falling

Cool name! This enchantment relates to boot armor. When it's equipped, it has the ability to cut back the damage you'll take from falling. Dropping like a noob from a cliff won't be so scary with this in use!

Bookshelves

Bookshelves, crafted from six planks and three books, can be placed around an enchantment table to increase the level requirement of enchantments to nine or higher. You need 15 bookshelves arranged around the table in a square.

Thorns

Any mob that goes for you with a melee or ranged attack could have some of the damage they cause you reflected back at them. Clever! It's added to your armor protection.

Sharpness

Want to make your sword or axe a little more terrifying? Going to power level V puts an extra damage point onto the weapon at level one, then 0.5 for each additional level.

Swift Sneak

Apply this to leggings, and you can move more quickly while sneaking or crawling. Can only be found in loot chests in Ancient Cities and is especially useful for moving in the deep dark.

Silk Touch

Some types of block, such as ores, don't drop themselves when mined—coal ore drops coal, and sculk drops nothing. Use Silk Touch on a tool and you can make the blocks drop themselves.

Frost Walker

This enchantment for boots has two benefits—it freezes water as you step on it, enabling you to walk across the surface, and confers immunity from stepping on magma and campfires.

Efficiency

Apply this to tools to increase your mining speed. You need to use the correct tool for a block to get the benefit—so axe on wood, pickaxe on stone and ore, etc.

Smite

This enchantment can be applied to swords and axes to increase damage to the undead. You can't use it in conjunction with Sharpness unless commands are used.

Luck of the Sea

Use this on a fishing rod to increase the chance of catching treasure while fishing. At level III, the chance goes from 55% to 11.5%, while the chance of catching junk goes down.

Piercing

This makes your arrows go through the target, which means they can also hit any mob standing behind them. The number of mobs that can be pierced with each arrow increases with each level.

Loyalty

This makes the trident an even more effective weapon, by making it return to you after you throw it. Casting at higher levels makes the trident return more speedily.

QUICK GUIDE TO
POTIONS

Follow these simple steps, and you'll soon know what's what in the complicated world of drinkable potions.

1 Essential Ingredients

Potions give you a status effect, such as night vision and strength, for a limited time. They are constructed on a **brewing stand** crafted with three cobblestone and one blaze rod. You also need a cauldron, bucket, blaze powder, and a glass bottle.

BREWING STAND

2 Base Facts

Before making a usable potion, you must create a base potion. Nether wart blocks (mined from soul sand in the Nether) make an "awkward" base potion. Add it to the top slot of the brewing stand above three water bottles.

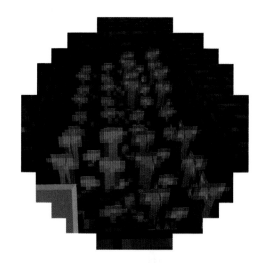

3 Secondary Potion

Awkward potions then need to be brewed with a secondary ingredient to form a secondary potion. Secondary ingredients include pufferfish, sugar, spider eyes, golden carrots, magma cream, ghast tears, and blaze powder—these last three mean a trip to the Nether!

DID YOU KNOW?

Splash potions can be chucked at an attacking mob to cause damage. With a normal potion in the bottles in your brewing stand, add gunpowder to the slot to brew a splash potion. Lingering potions are similar and create a cloud after exploding from being thrown.

4 Mod to Measure

A modifying ingredient, such as redstone or gunpowder, can be brewed with the secondary potion. Now you're ready to start brewing potions that can do good and bad things! Don't worry if it takes a long time to understand this process. It's difficult, so you'll make mistakes and learn along the way. Ask a friend who is more experienced for help if needed.

POPULAR POTIONS

Check out these crucial potions that you can use to get an advantage over your opponents as you become a better Minecrafter . . .

Night Vision

If you're battling mobs at night, use the night vision potion to see what's actually going on. It won't be effective against boss mobs, but for three minutes, it gives you the ability to turn night into day . . . well, almost!

Strength

This only applies to melee-attacking situations, but get this lovely liquid inside you, and the damage you can deal to monsters is increased by three. That's a big difference in combat.

Leaping

In Minecraft, your ambitions should be sky-high. This potion won't actually help you reach the clouds, but it will give you a jump boost that will see you leap over small obstacles in just one attempt. Awesome!

Healing

Different to regeneration, the healing potion rewards the user with an instant hit of four health points. It's a favorite potion for use in the Nether, where plenty of creepy creatures are on the attack.

!

DID YOU KNOW?

If you're lucky, potions, cauldrons, and brewing stands can be found naturally around the dimensions.

Poison

Obviously, don't use this one on yourself! Poison should be thrown as a splash potion to dish out damage for 45 seconds. It can't kill, but it proves an effective weapon against most mobs.

Regeneration

Give your depleted health bar a major uplift by downing this potion to see those lovely red hearts start to fill up again over time. If you take a sudden impact to your health, this item can be a lifesaver!

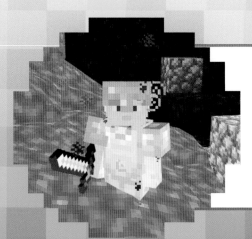

Fire Resistance

Drink this to give yourself three minutes of protection against fire damage (such as lava and magma blocks). If you are venturing to the Nether, this is a great tool to have on hand.

STEP 14— NEW HEIGHTS AND DEPTHS

The highest and deepest regions of Minecraft are some of the most fascinating for players to explore. A sequence of updates made to the game in 2021 and 2022 introduced lots of new features based around underground regions and mountains—or "Caves and Cliffs" as the first update was called.

PEAK PERFORMANCE

**You thought you'd seen mountains before?
These are *real* mountains . . .**

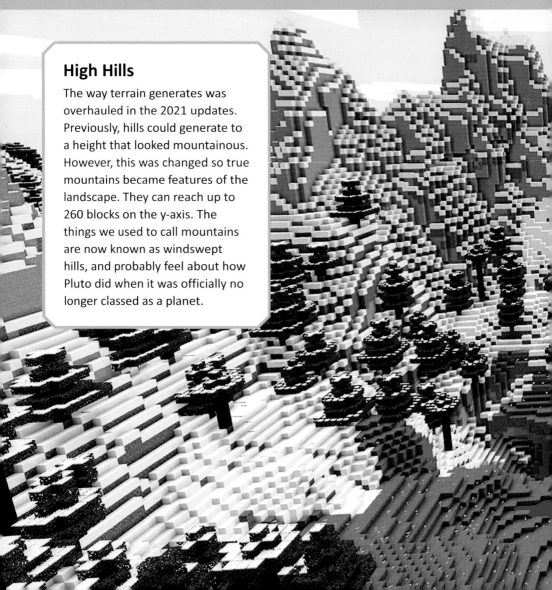

High Hills

The way terrain generates was overhauled in the 2021 updates. Previously, hills could generate to a height that looked mountainous. However, this was changed so true mountains became features of the landscape. They can reach up to 260 blocks on the y-axis. The things we used to call mountains are now known as windswept hills, and probably feel about how Pluto did when it was officially no longer classed as a planet.

On the Up

Mountains have their own sub-biomes. The meadow biome generates around the foot of a mountain, as well as on plateaus (that's a flat area of land partway up a mountain). A grove is a forest on the slope of a mountain and generates at higher altitudes. Snowy slopes are more featureless and generate on the sides of mountains. Then there are three types of peak biome: jagged, frozen, and stony. These biomes will only generate at the top of a mountain. Jagged ones are made of stone with a single layer of snow. Frozen ones tend to be smoother, with packed ice underneath. And stony peaks are warmer, without the covering of ice and snow.

Take a Peak

Peaks and snowy slopes are the only places in the game where goats spawn. Mountains are also a great source of iron, emerald, and coal ore—especially if you travel up to the peaks.

GET ON DOWN

Caves have always been a big feature of Minecraft, but they now stretch deeper than ever before . . .

Caves generate as low as -59 on the y-axis, and finding one can save you time and effort when mining ores. Often ore will be exposed on cave walls and is found with greater frequency as you go deeper. However, there's also a higher chance of encountering hostile mobs in these dark regions.

Not Too Close

There are two main types of cave. Carvers are caves generated the traditional way, block by block, using terrain generation rules. They can come in several different sizes. Noise caves are made using a noise generator—basically, a random mass of pixels which the program then examines to find patterns. A cheese cave is generated by looking for blobs in the randomness, like the holes in Swiss cheese. A spaghetti cave is generated by looking for paths through the randomness and joining them up, like strings of spaghetti. These two patterns can be combined to form a cave system where the large caverns of the cheese caves are connected by the narrower passages of the spaghetti caves.

Drip Feeding

Like mountains, caves have their own unique sub-biomes. Dripstone caves tend to generate a long way from oceans, with small pools of water and lots of stalagmites and stalactites. Dripstone block forms here. Lush caves generate beneath warmer, more humid biomes and contain cave vines, dripleaf, spore blossom, and glow berries. They're also home to axolotls, glow squids, and tropical fish. And then there's the deep dark . . .

WHOA, THAT'S DEEP

. . . and dark. The deep dark biome is perhaps the most mysterious in Minecraft . . .

The deep dark is a cave biome that generates rarely, and always deep underground. It's most likely to be found underneath plateaus or mountain peaks and is filled with a type of block called sculk.

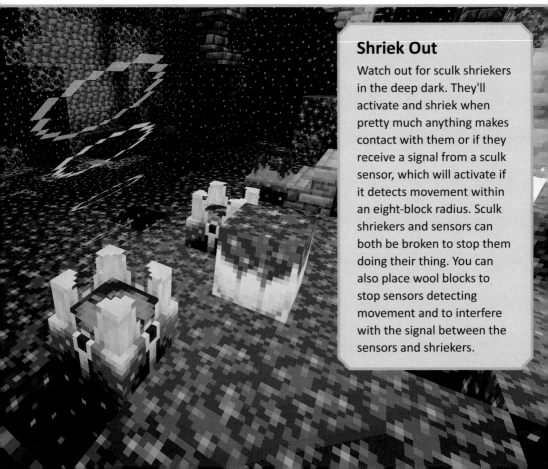

Shriek Out

Watch out for sculk shriekers in the deep dark. They'll activate and shriek when pretty much anything makes contact with them or if they receive a signal from a sculk sensor, which will activate if it detects movement within an eight-block radius. Sculk shriekers and sensors can both be broken to stop them doing their thing. You can also place wool blocks to stop sensors detecting movement and to interfere with the signal between the sensors and shriekers.

This Means Warden

The warden is a hostile mob that only spawns in the deep dark, and instead of the usual spawning mechanism, it spawns from the ground after the player has set off four sculk shriekers. It looks kind of like an iron golem—but it's actually the toughest mob in the game, with the highest melee damage and the highest health. It's blind, and uses its sense of hearing and smell to fight. Oh, and its sonic boom attacks can get through enchanted armor, and nearly anything else you might use to reduce damage. Have fun!

DID YOU KNOW?

Shriekers and wardens both cause the player to suffer from Darkness—a condition that makes your vision go dim.

ANCIENT CITIES

Mysterious structures built thousands of years before Minecraft was even invented!

In the deep dark biome, at depths of -51, Ancient Cities can generate. They look like ruined palaces filled with crumbling columns, walls, and steps, strongly influenced by Roman and Mayan ruins. Rooms that make up an Ancient City include barracks, chambers, ice boxes (which contain ice and note blocks), and saunas (containing small rectangular pools). They're mostly composed of deepslate in various forms, though one type of room—known as a camp—contains wool in shades of blue.

Tomb Raiding

When looking for chests, saunas are the best places to search—each one should contain three chests. Also, pretty much any building with upper levels will have a chest or two up there: these loot-filled structures are officially known as tall ruins. And you can definitely find some awesome loot in these chests, some of which can't be found anywhere else. The only enchanted books to contain Swift Sneak reside in Ancient Cities, for instance, and the spell is particularly useful for avoiding sensors and shriekers in the deep dark. These are also the only places you can find echo shards, which are essential for crafting a recovery compass.

Secret Circuits

An Ancient City will have a structure at its center—a giant frame that looks like a warden's head. At the base of it, you'll find the entrance to a network of hidden basements, which contain redstone circuits.

SCULKING AROUND THE DEEP

Go deep underground, and you'll find two interesting materials: sculk and deepslate . . .

Sculk is exclusively found in the deep dark. We've already mentioned shriekers and sensors, but sculk also forms as a basic block—a dark turquoise material with glowing spots that don't actually give out light—and as a thin layer on the surface of other blocks. The best way to mine it is with a hoe.

Ashes to Ashes, Sculk to Sculk

A sculk catalyst is a type of sculk block that generates more sculk. When a mob dies within an eight-block radius of a sculk catalyst, a patch of sculk forms: blocks are replaced by sculk, and sculk veins form across the surface of other blocks.

Rock Solid

When you go lower than 8 on the y-axis, you'll start to find stone is replaced by deepslate, a darker form of stone that takes twice as long to break. By the time you hit zero, deepslate will have taken over from stone and will be the dominant type of block. Furthermore, any ore that spawns inside it will spawn as a deepslate variant of that ore. This means there are deepslate versions of coal, copper, diamond, emerald, gold, iron, lapis lazuli, and redstone. These variants take 1.5 times longer to break than the regular versions and unfortunately don't have any extra benefits.

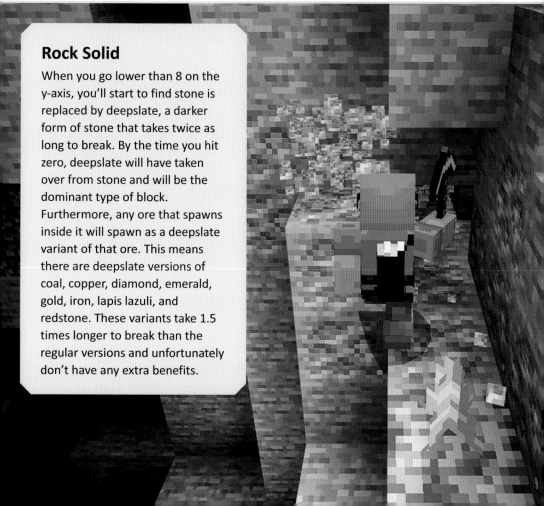

STEP 15— NAVIGATE THE NETHER

Delving into the Nether is not for the faint-hearted! It's a terrifying, dark, and dangerous dimension, full of angry mobs, lava, magma, and fire that will cause you mega damage. One day, though, you'll need to make this journey. Be brave and check out the following pages for everything you need to know, from piglins to the deadly basalt deltas!

REASONS TO EXPLORE
THE NETHER!

Come on, let's take your gameplay to another dimension. Discover what lurks inside this evil area, as well as what makes it a must-visit place!

Essential Resources

To put it simply, you just can't reach the End unless you first explore the Nether. This dimension has an ingredient called Nether wart, which grows in the Nether and is found in chests. This ingredient is needed in potions. Blaze powder comes from a blaze rod, which is dropped by blazes in the Nether. It's needed for potions and crafting eye of ender.

Extra Experience

Mining Nether quartz ore from within netherrack will give you plenty of XP, which then helps you to level up in the Nether. This quartz is used in lots of redstone recipes. Netherrack dominates the Nether dimension and will burn forever once it's set on fire—it's a great way to cut down on using torches!

More Mobs

This place is as hostile as it gets! Blazes, zombie pigmen, and even magma cubes all hang out here.

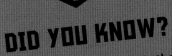

DID YOU KNOW?

The wither is summoned in the Nether, by placing four soul sand blocks in a T-shape with three wither skeleton skulls on top. When defeated, its dropped nether star can be crafted into a beacon to give out helpful status effects.

THE NETHER PORTAL

It's the only way to enter the Nether—and to get you back again to the safety of the Overworld. Check out what this magical doorway is all about . . .

End Portal

Unlike End portals and exit portals, Nether portals are built upright. You can build one in the Overworld to transport you into the Nether. When you appear in the Nether, there will be a portal there to whisk you back again—something you'll probably do frequently as a new visitor to this dark place.

Craft a Portal

A portal is made with 10 obsidian blocks. Obsidian is mined near the Overworld's base, where moving water meets lava. Obsidian can't be collected in the Nether, so take it with you if you want to build another portal there. Place the obsidian blocks to make a portal frame like this. You can make a complete rectangle and fill in the corners if you like, but this isn't required, and it does need four more obsidian blocks!

Light It Up!

The portal now needs a fire inside it to be activated. The quickest way is to use flint and steel, but fire charges and an arrow with flame enchantment will also achieve this. The blocks in the middle will twinkle purple to show that the portal is open and ready!

DID YOU KNOW?

Traveling one block in the Nether is the same as going eight in the Overworld. It's possible to move big distances quickly by walking in the Nether, then using a portal to propel you to the Overworld in a completely different spot.

In Survival, a player needs to stand in a portal for four seconds to then be carried into the Nether.

FEARSOME FORTRESS

Packed with corridors, bridges, balconies and staircases, the Nether fortress rewards careful exploration.

Get Comfortable

Follow bridge paths to take you into the fortress. It's big and creepy! Get used to being here so that you can mine helpful things like Nether wart and glowstone. Nether brick and Nether brick fence can also be mined, but the fences don't burn like general wooden fences do.

DID YOU KNOW?

Fortunately, the huge ghast mobs do not spawn in Nether fortresses.

Blaze

Watch out for blaze spawner blocks! Blaze mobs appear from here when the light is below 12. Listen out for the terrifying deep breathing sounds they make—deal with them quickly, and collect dropped blaze rods.

Find the Fortress

A fortress is still a good place to make a protective base. Use cobblestone to make a small shelter to hide you from mobs, adding an iron door with a button-opening system to keep mobs out. Separate shelters can become a place for potions and enchantments.

Light Your Way

Keep a fortress well lit using torches or glowstone, or by burning netherrack. Mobs such as wither skeleton and enderman won't appreciate that, but ghasts and magma cubes can spawn in any light level.

NETHER KNOWLEDGE

Here are some of the blocks, items, and mobs you can expect to find in the Nether.

Bridge Paths

Follow bridge paths to take you into the fortress. It's big and creepy! Get used to being in there so that you can mine helpful things like Nether wart and glowstone. Nether brick and Nether brick fence can also be mined, but the fences don't burn like general wooden fences do.

Hogging Your Attention

Piglins and hoglins are hostile mobs that love to attack on sight! Piglins are known to attack hoglins, and they both hang around in the Crimson Forest biome. Piglins adore gold and may trade it with you for other items.

Growing Greens

The Nether has its own vegetation, including Nether sprouts, warped roots, and crimson roots. Crimson fungi and warped fungi can also be grown. Bone meal will help this, and adding bone meal on Netherrack will promote nylium.

Bastion Remnants

These fascinating castle-like structures generate naturally in all parts of the Nether except the basalt deltas. There are four types of bastion remnant: bridges, hoglin stables, housing units, and treasure rooms. You can find unique loot inside, such as magma cube spawners, gilded blackstone, and the pigstep music disc. Crying obsidian and enchanted gold armor also have a chance of appearing in chests.

NETHER BIOMES

The Nether is a long way from normal, and, no surprise, it has sub-biomes you won't find anywhere else . . .

There are five Nether biomes—and due to its hell-like nature, all of them are dry. They also have the same temperature—2.0, the same as desert and badlands biomes. You can't place water here. You can place ice—but packed ice and blue ice never melt. Weird.

Nether Wastes

This is the main Nether biome, made up mostly of netherrack and lava lakes. This is the place to look for the rare block known as ancient debris, which has a very high blast resistance. Clusters of glowstone blobs are commonly found here.

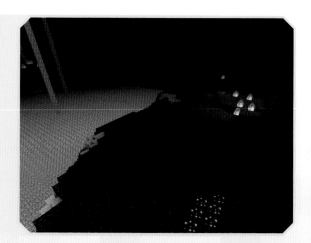

Soul Sand Valley

As the name suggests, this biome is mostly composed of soul sand and soul soil. The main characteristic of soul blocks is they slow down any player or mob that moves across them. (This can be counteracted by the Soul Speed enchantment.)

Warped Forest

This is more chill than other Nether biomes, because far fewer mobs spawn in it—just occasional endermen and striders, plus any that spawn in fortresses or bastion remnants. Instead of trees, the forest is made up of huge warped fungus. Warped nylium makes up the ground.

Crimson Forest

Similar to the warped forest, the crimson forest is home to huge crimson fungus. A dark red fog hangs over it. It's a more hostile environment than the warped forest because hoglins and piglins spawn here. The dominant block is crimson nylium, which drops netherrack when mined.

Basalt Deltas

This biome is filled with lava, including deltas which are sheets of lava one block deep. Basalt columns can generate here—groups of basalt towers, which can contain pools of lava in between. This biome isn't common, but it's very dangerous—look out for leaping magma cubes!

10 TOP TIPS!

Want to catch up on some random but super-helpful hints and tips for surviving in the Nether? Then read on, Minecrafters!

1 Portal Placement

Some mobs can use a Nether portal, so don't build it next to your base just in case a monster travels from the Nether and appears right next to you! Some experienced Minecrafters like to place the portal in a big hole in the ground to help keep any escaped mobs at bay.

2 Mushroom Stew

Before the Nether update came along, mushrooms were the only naturally growing food in the Nether. Crafted in a recipe with a bowl, they can produce mushroom stew and restore six hunger for a tasty boost in the dark dimension.

3 Bed Blast

Fancy a little rest? Think again. If you do try to sleep in a bed in the Nether, it will explode and cause more damage than a TNT explosion! Beds do not work as a respawn point here, and you'll leave the Nether after you die.

4

Time Trap

Be aware that clocks are useless in the dark and dismal Nether. There are no readings from a compass either, and you'll be clueless as to what part of day or night it is. Time just seems to magically stand still in here, and that can be quite unsettling.

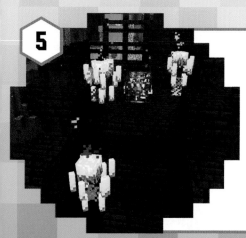

5

Group Force

A blaze is a difficult mob to defeat. Not only does it detect you if you're in a 48-block range, but if you do inflict damage, they can summon all other blazes within that zone to gang up on you! Yikes.

6 Mega Minecarts

A minecart system in the Nether can transport you and items quickly around the Nether. They can move up and down steep hills. This requires rails, powered rails, and a minecart to be crafted—it's tricky, but it's worth spending the resources and time.

7 Light Up

Now you can make burning fire appear with an impressive blue flame in the Nether. The soul soil block burns this cool color when set alight—it doesn't spread like normal fire but deals more damage!

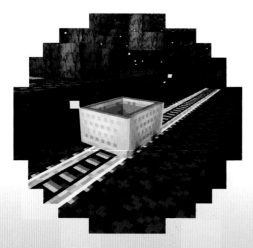

8 A Quick Buck

Made with just three iron ingots, the simple bucket will become a handy inventory item when you're in the Nether. It can be equipped to take away a surprise lava source, which you're bound to discover as you delve into the netherrack.

9

Supersize

The minimum number of obsidian needed for a portal is 10 (in a 4x5 scale), but in fact, it can be made much, much bigger. It would be a waste of precious resources to do this—however, you can take it to 23x23 and leave a massive 21x21 opening in which to reach the Nether.

10

Nether Get Knocked

You've already heard how the new Netherite material is even stronger than diamond, which means that Netherite armor makes you totally tough. It provides a huge barrier to any knockback, while ammunition will hardly give you a scratch.

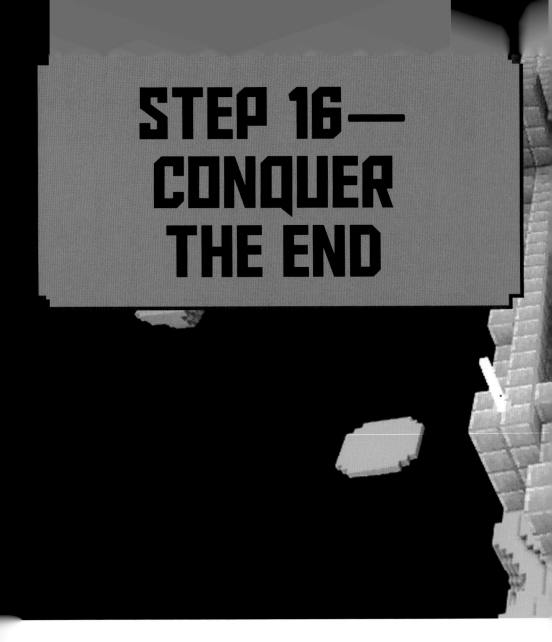

STEP 16— CONQUER THE END

Things such as the end crystals, endermen, obsidian, potions, portals, islands, and of course, the famous and fearsome ender dragon are all part of the exciting endeavor in Minecraft Survival! The End requires nerves of steel and a command of top fighting tactics to be able to master it. Ready for a final challenge? Turn the page, and take a trip you'll never forget.

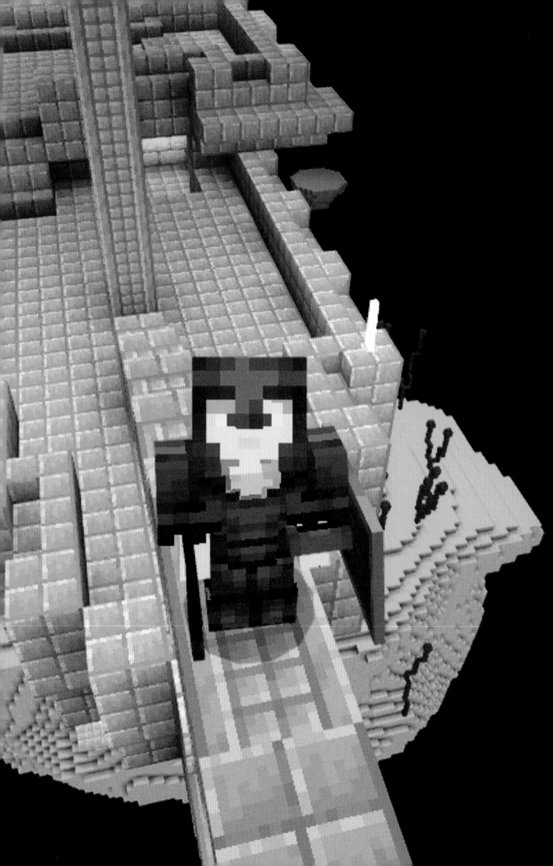

THE END . . .
AT THE START!

Learn the ins and outs of what's required before you enter the End, plus some essential info on what it's like.

Get Ready

A lot needs to happen in your game and world before you can think of exploring the End. You will need to have crafted a diamond pickaxe and mined obsidian for the Nether portal, collected blaze rods and defeated endermen for their ender pearls. Phew!

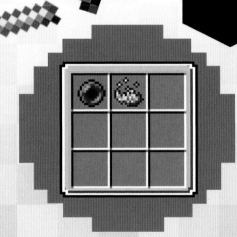

End Portal

Ender pearls also exist in chests in the stronghold structure (see more on pages 184—85). One ender pearl and one blaze powder combine in a recipe to create eye of ender. Eyes of ender are needed to help you find a stronghold, and you need as many as 12 more to activate the end portal inside it. An end portal gives you the only route to reach the End.

What Do You Need in the End?

First of all, you need to be prepared! Have armor, shield, strong weapons, obsidian for shelter, dirt blocks to climb on, water buckets to tackle any endermen, and plenty of potions, splash potions, enchantments, and food in your inventory. It takes a lot of exploring and adventures in both the Overworld and Nether, so you won't be visiting the End until you're truly an epic Minecrafter!

What Does the End Look Like?

Made of end stone, the End is a collection of dark islands that are surrounded by the Void. Located around 1,000 blocks from these is the central island—home of the mega-evil ender dragon! Here, you'll see tall obsidian towers with end crystals (previously called ender crystals) placed on top. Some of these are encased in iron bars.

CRACKING A STRONGHOLD

**Finding a stronghold is a mighty mission in itself!
Follow these tips for locating and learning
what strongholds are all about.**

Finding . . .

The first step toward finding an underground stronghold from the Overworld is throwing an eye of ender. It moves towards the direction of a stronghold, then hits the ground. If that eye of ender hasn't broken, throw it again, or throw a new eye. Repeat this move so that eventually all eyes fall on the same location—this marks where you must dig to reach a stronghold.

Exploring . . .

Walk around the stronghold's corridors, and you may discover helpful loot chests, fountain rooms with water, and other valuable resources. What you're really after, though, is an end portal room and the portal inside it. To activate the portal, place eyes of ender in the 12 frame slots around it (some may be filled already), and then step inside it.

Watch Out!

Watch out for silverfish mobs around end portal rooms. These little monsters can be a big pain, and quick melee skills with a sword can be effective in defeating them. It's also a very good idea to have a bed here as a respawn point and plenty of supplies stashed in chests.

DID YOU KNOW?

Silverfish disguise themselves as blocks, so be careful when you mine because you may unleash them by mistake.

THE DEADLY DRAGON!

Packed with awesome attacking moves and a scary level of health, this boss mob is the ultimate enemy!

Meet the Ender Dragon

The ender dragon has 200 health. Once you appear in the central island from your portal, it won't take long for you to see it swoop into action! The ender dragon draws its mighty power from the end crystals—these must be destroyed! Use a bow to do this safely from a distance. You can climb the obsidian towers using dirt blocks, but it's a risky strategy.

Ender Charges

In its arsenal are powerful fireballs called ender charges. Mixed with its potent breath, these form purple clouds when they touch you and make damage. Since it's a flying mob, bows and crossbows are the best way to inflict damage on this

beast. If you're brave, a sword swipe in close melee attacks can cause the ender dragon harm, but make sure you quickly jump out of its way again. Fire and lava won't cause it any distress!

"Sleep" Attack

A clever way to inflict fatal blows is to place a bed, then attempt to sleep in it and cause the bed to explode (like it does in the Nether, too). If you then shield behind obsidian, the blast can do a lot of damage to the dragon but you'll be protected.

Endermen

Endermen will be on the attack in these chaotic scenes as well, so wearing a pumpkin to keep them calm is wise. It will take all of your expert combat skills, potions, enchanted armor and further enchantments to take it down. When the dragon's sitting on the small central podium, it can't be struck by arrows but will still take sword damage.

Night Vision

Use the night vision potion from page 182 to see the dragon against the void.

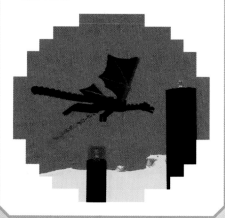

Keep Fighting!

Keep fighting hard and using all of your abilities to finally see the ultimate boss mob defeated!

THE END IS HERE

Wow! So now that the dragon is history, is it really the end of your Minecraft Survival adventure? Well, yes and no . . . the fun can still continue.

What Now?

With that sweet success of defeating the ender dragon, you may want to rest for a few minutes and take in the incredible achievement! You will see that the exit portal has magically appeared, along with the dragon egg—this is the biggest trophy you can take in Minecraft. The exit portal now lets you travel between the End and the Overworld.

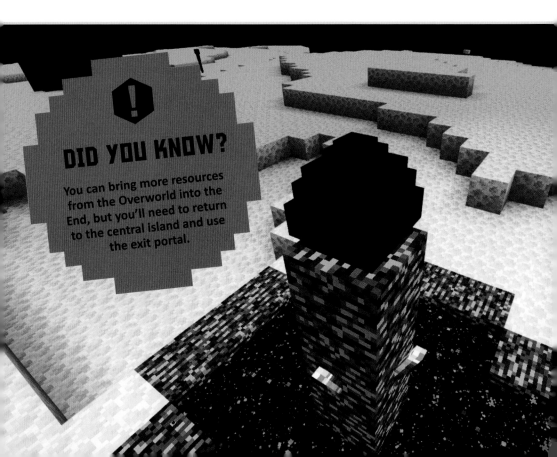

! DID YOU KNOW?

You can bring more resources from the Overworld into the End, but you'll need to return to the central island and use the exit portal.

Round 2

Maybe you've developed a taste for taking on the dragon and fancy your fighting chances once again? Well, you can actually make the ender dragon respawn by placing four end crystals around the exit portal, with one on each side. Craft end crystals with seven glass blocks, an eye of ender, and a ghast tear.

Outer Islands

If you want to tour the End's outer islands and see what's on offer there, go through the end gateway portal by placing an ender pearl in it and then teleporting. Just try not to get lost on your journey! You'll also need to build bridges from the islands to keep you from falling into the Void.

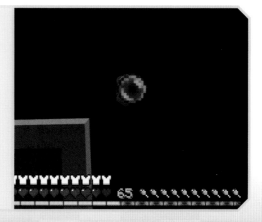

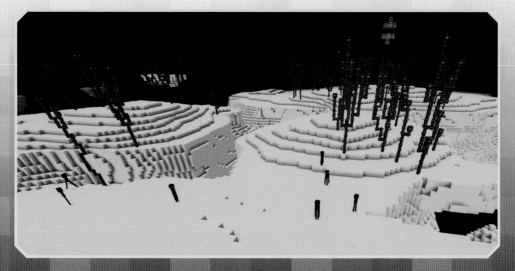

MUCH MORE MINECRAFT

The excitement and exploration never needs to stop in the wonderful world of Survival!

Keep your Minecraft journey moving in the End, and with some exploration of the outer islands, End cities should soon appear. These large, naturally generated structures are mega mysterious, and their purple appearance makes them stand out. Tall raised towers are joined by pathways that lead to tower rooms. Here, chests can be found, and perhaps you'll see the end rods, which are a new form of light.

You've seen how vast, creative, and fun Minecraft is. It's an exciting world that you can master with practice and a clever use of tactics to keep up with the challenges it offers. Keep enjoying the adventure!

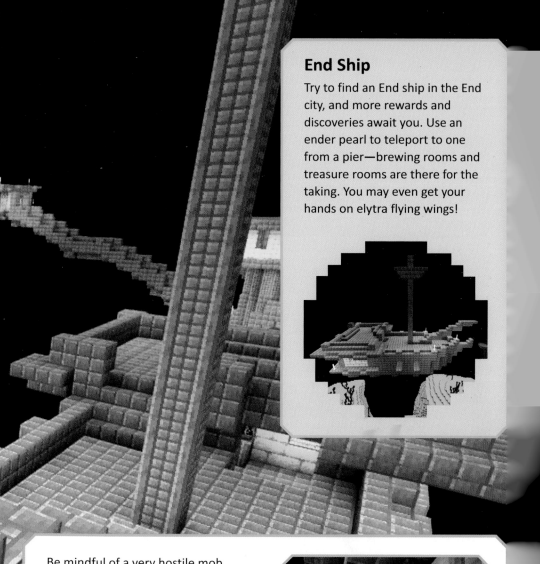

End Ship

Try to find an End ship in the End city, and more rewards and discoveries await you. Use an ender pearl to teleport to one from a pier—brewing rooms and treasure rooms are there for the taking. You may even get your hands on elytra flying wings!

Be mindful of a very hostile mob called the shulker. An enchanted diamond sword is often the answer to these tormentors that hide themselves among the blocks. They can pick you up within 16 blocks and team up to take you on! Defeat one, and the dropped shell can be used to create a 27-storage block shulker box. What new mobs may appear in the End in the future?

HOW TO BEAT MINECRAFT

Check off each step as you master it!

STEP 1	>>> GET STARTED	☐
STEP 2	>>> OVERWORLD OVERLOAD	☐
STEP 3	>>> SURVIVE 24 HOURS	☐
STEP 4	>>> KEEP CRAFTING	☐
STEP 5	>>> GET MINING	☐
STEP 6	>>> BUILD BETTER SHELTERS	☐
STEP 7	>>> FARM FOR RESOURCES	☐
STEP 8	>>> STAY FED	☐
STEP 9	>>> WATCH OUT FOR WILDLIFE	☐
STEP 10	>>> TAKE ON HOSTILE MOBS	☐
STEP 11	>>> BE A MASTER OF COMBAT	☐
STEP 12	>>> SOURCE YOUR ARMOR!	☐
STEP 13	>>> USE MAGIC	☐
STEP 14	>>> NEW HEIGHTS AND DEPTHS	☐
STEP 15	>>> NAVIGATE THE NETHER	☐
STEP 16	>>> CONQUER THE END	☐

THIS PLAYER HAS REACHED A HIGHER LEVEL. THIS PLAYER IS STRONGER
THAN THEY REALIZE. THIS PLAYER IS YOU!